A
TURNED-ON CHURCH
IN AN
UPTIGHT WORLD

A TURNED-ON CHURCH IN AN UPTIGHT WORLD

A STUDY GUIDE ON FIRST CORINTHIANS
WITH QUESTIONS FOR DISCUSSION GROUPS

C. PETER WAGNER

ZONDERVAN PUBLISHING HOUSE
A DIVISION OF THE ZONDERVAN CORPORATION
GRAND RAPIDS, MICHIGAN

A TURNED-ON CHURCH IN AN UPTIGHT WORLD
© 1971 C. Peter Wagner

Second printing   May 1972
Third printing   November 1972

Library of Congress Catalog Card Number 77-156241

Unless otherwise indicated, the Scripture references in this book are taken from *The Modern Language Bible, The New Berkeley Version in Modern English.* © 1945, 1959, 1969 by the Zondervan Publishing House. Grand Rapids, Michigan.

Printed in the United States of America

To our children:

KAREN

RUTH

REBECCA

this book is affectionately

dedicated

Table of Contents

Foreword

Missionaries are not expected to be fully abreast of developments on the home front, but Peter Wagner obviously is. Although Bolivia has been his field since 1956, he writes with keen perceptiveness of the needs of our churches at home and abroad, applying the lessons of First Corinthians to the current scene.

He writes with skill and forthrightness in vigorous, colorful language. No reader will be able to stifle his curiosity piqued by the highly original chapter headings. Lured on, he will find plenty of food for thought in the brief, hard-hitting expositions which unfold the major topics discussed by the Apostle Paul.

The author is concerned to detect in the errors of the Corinthians various pitfalls facing the modern church. His book is not intended to explore the byways of the text as a verse-by-verse commentary would do, but rather seeks to follow the highway blazed by Paul in his efforts to deliver a first-century congregation from its carnality and misconceptions.

Because of its readability and practicality, this volume would be an excellent manual for church study groups desirous of improving the quality of their congregational life.

EVERETT F. HARRISON

Fuller Theological Seminary

Preface

This book, hopefully, is not another conventional commentary on First Corinthians. It is far from a verse-by-verse explanation of the book. Instead it is a series of twelve essays which are based on the main teachings of Paul in his epistle. Rather than being called a general introduction to First Corinthians, the term "general orientation" might fit better.

I first became aware of the tremendous implications of First Corinthians for the contemporary church while I was a student at Fuller Seminary many years ago. It was not in the classroom, but rather in a weekly Bible study at Lake Avenue Congregational Church where Dr. Charles Woodbridge taught the book, that I became fascinated by its teaching. As seminary learning progressed, I had the privilege of reading First Corinthians in Greek with Dr. Everett Harrison. The Berean Class of Bell Friends Church graciously endured the experience of hearing me teach it the first time. Since then I have been through the book with several classes in the Emmaus Bible Institute (now the George Allan Theological Seminary) and the Baptist Theological Seminary, both in Cochabamba. Upon the generous invitation of Pastor Clayton Schletewitz I was recently able to give the studies again at Bell Friends Church some fourteen years after the first attempt. In the meantime I had published the studies as a series of articles in *Eternity* in English and in *Visión Evangélica* and *Pensamiento Cristiano* in Spanish. The latest occasion for open discussion of the ideas presented in this book took place in the Monday evening prayer meeting of the Andes Evangelical Mission in Cochabamba. Fellow workers helped smooth some rough edges and offered many new ideas.

Almost a decade and a half of missionary experience has contributed toward a special understanding of what Paul, as a missionary, wrote to one of his national churches. Whereas not much new truth may be uncovered in this book, at least the reader will probably see First Corinthians from a slightly different point of view from that which would be taken by a non-missionary writer.

I would like to express my gratitude to the individuals already mentioned, to Russell Hitt and William Peterson of *Eternity* for their permission to use articles published in that magazine as a basis for this book, and to my wife, Doris, for typing the manuscript and preparing it for publication.

C. Peter Wagner

Cochabamba, Bolivia

* * *

This Preface must have an appendix. Few unpublished manuscripts have been prayed over as much as this one. I came to Pasadena from Bolivia to teach at the School of World Mission in early January, 1970, leaving the original manuscript with my wife for her to type and send to the publisher before she joined me in late February. However, she fell ill, underwent major surgery, and could not finish the job. So she brought the only existing manuscript and all that she had typed with her in her suitcase. Then the airline proceeded to lose the suitcase!

For three weeks and a day the Fuller Seminary faculty and staff, the student body, the West Coast Council of the Andes Evangelical Mission, and the congregations of Bell Friends Church and Granada Heights Friends Church prayed fervently for the lost suitcase. Then just three days before we left to return to Bolivia, the suitcase was delivered at 10:30 P.M. Praise the Lord!

Outline

Since the essays on the different sections of First Corinthians do not rigidly follow the logical outline of the book, this general outline is presented for the reader who wishes to refer to it. It is admitted that the "difficulty-doctrine-decision" scheme for dividing each section is often more pedagogical than exegetical.

I. INTRODUCTION TO THE EPISTLE (1:1-9)
   A. The author (1:1)
   B. The recipients (1:2)
   C. The salutation (1:3)
   D. The virtues of the church (1:4-9)

II. DIVISIONS IN THE CHURCH (CHAPTERS 1-4)
   A. Difficulty (1:10-17)
      1. Divisions (1:10)
      2. Contentions (1:11)
      3. The four parties (1:12)
   B. Doctrine (1:18—3:4)
      1. False wisdom (1:18—2:5)
      2. True wisdom (2:6-13)
      3. Carnality the cause (2:14—3:4)
   C. Decision (3:5—4:21)
      1. Cooperation (3:5-9)
      2. Confidence in the Holy Spirit (3:16, 17)
      3. Not judging our brethren (3:10-15, 18—4:21)

III. CHURCH DISCIPLINE (CHAPTERS 5, 6)
    A. Difficulty (5:1, 2)
        1. Immorality
        2. The attitude of the church
    B. Doctrine (5:6-13; 6:9-21)
        1. The leavening of Passover (5:6-8)
        2. Separation (5:9-13)
        3. The carnal solution (6:1-8)
        4. Moral purity (6:9-20)
    C. Decision (5:3-5, 13b)
        1. Correction of the brother (5:5)
        2. Protection of the church (5:7)

IV. MARRIAGE (CHAPTER 7)
    A. Difficulty
    B. Doctrine
        1. The purity of marriage (7:1-9)
        2. The permanence of marriage (7:10, 11)
        3. The power of marriage (7:12-16)
        4. The privilege of celibacy (7:17-40)
    C. Decision

V. CHRISTIAN LIBERTY (CHAPTERS 8-10)
    A. Difficulty (8:1)
    B. Doctrine (8:1—10:24)
        1. Basic principles of Christian liberty (8:1-13)
        2. Illustrations of the doctrine (9:1—10:15)
            a. Paul himself (9:1-27)
            b. Israel (10:1-15)
        3. Contrast between Christian and pagan feasts (10:16-22)
    C. Decision (10:20-33)

VI. CHRISTIAN WORSHIP (CHAPTER 11)
    A. Difficulty
        1. The position of the woman (11:2-16)
        2. The Lord's Supper (11:17-34)

A
TURNED-ON CHURCH
IN AN
UPTIGHT WORLD

1

The Gospel in a Sex-Saturated Society

Acts 18

TODAY'S LOVE-INS, key clubs, Playboy bunnies, nudist colonies, erotic movies, gay bars, and four-letter words in otherwise dignified magazines sometimes make us think that we live in history's most sex-saturated society. There have been others, however. Take Sodom. Or Corinth.

For the Greeks and Romans of the first century, "to corinthianize" was a naughty thirteen-letter word. In a broad sense it meant "go to the devil"; more specifically it meant "to fornicate." As bad as countries like the United States or Sweden are today, they probably are not yet up to (or down to!) ancient Corinth. History tells us that at one time Corinth boasted 1,000 sacred prostitutes serving the temple of the goddess Aphrodite alone. For thousands of Corinthians to worship their god was to patronize the "priestesses."

If this is the way the Corinthians took their religion, it does not require much imagination to guess what the rest of their daily lives was like. Sin of all kinds and descriptions had free rein among them.

One factor which contributed to Corinth's deep dive into the cesspool of immorality was the stream of commerce pouring through the city. Located on the isthmus which joined mainland Greece to the southern peninsula, it was a

19

major seaport town. Merchants preferred to transport their goods overland through Corinth rather than risk the hazardous journey around the rocky southern coast of Achaia. The waterfront anywhere in the world is always a tough neighborhood. Corinth teemed with sailors of all nationalities far from home. When they landed in Corinth they were looking for a good time. The pagan Corinthians were more than ready to provide them everything they were seeking.

Can the Gospel of Christ do anything in such a sex-saturated society?

In spite of Corinth's bad reputation, in many ways the city was ripe for the Gospel. True, not everyone there was ready to repent of his sin and trust Christ, but certain conditions prevailed that predisposed a segment of the population toward Christianity. The Holy Spirit had prepared the ground and had called the apostle Paul, one of God's choice missionaries and evangelists, to the right place at the right time.

One of the historical factors that opened the door to Corinth was the process of destruction and rebuilding. Corinth had passed through a long history as a city, but it was completely destroyed by the Romans in 146 B.C. The Corinthians who survived the destruction were sold into slavery. For 100 years nothing was there, until Caesar rebuilt the city in 46 B.C. This means that the deep-rooted traditions, social structures, cultural values, and vested interests which characterize older cities and civilizations did not exist in Corinth. When the apostle Paul arrived in A.D. 51, the city was just over 100 years old, relatively young as cities go. The population was a mixed, heterogeneous crowd, vigorous and spirited. In general the Corinthians were open to new ideas and new experiences. In this respect they were quite the opposite of their neighbors in Athens, for the people there were proud, sophisticated, and steeped in binding religious and philosophical traditions.

Only recently have missionaries and evangelists been

awakening to the fact that the Holy Spirit throughout history has used certain types of social and political conditions to prepare the soil for the sowing of the Gospel and the planting of churches. The development of new sciences such as sociology and anthropology for the first time have placed at our fingertips the analytical categories within which patterns can be discovered. Even computers can be called in to help evangelistic strategy-planning today. One of the lessons which those who establish new churches have learned is that wherever people are in social flux, separated from ancient customs and fixed social relationships, they are more apt to be receptive to the Gospel. United States church history illustrates this clearly. As the nation pushed west, the people on the frontier were almost invariably more receptive to the Gospel than those in the older eastern cities. This is one reason why in ancient Greece Corinth was more receptive than Athens.

Corinth's sex-saturation, ironically, was another factor which helped prepare many of its citizens for Christianity. Illicit sex, as most sin, puts up a beautiful front. Opportunities for fornication and adultery call into action a bodily hormone release so powerful that a person's moral vision is instantly shortened. Rather than seeing the long-term moral implications of the temptation, he becomes myopic enough to place great value upon the immediate pleasure and satisfaction that sex offers. The next half hour often seems more important than the next five years.

There is no need to deny that illicit sex produces pleasure. If it didn't, it would have gone out of style long ago. But there is good reason to deny that pleasure derived from this type of activity, or any form of hedonism, is a life value to be sought after and treasured by any man. Sex was created by God with two dimensions, the physiological and the spiritual. The physiological dimension can be experienced in any bedroom, brothel or back seat. But this is only half-sex. The other half is the complete, permanent, no-strings-attached commitment in love that two people make to each other in the marriage vows. No one can play with only the first dimension of sex and hope to find more than an immediate and fleeting satisfaction. God has arranged sin in such a way that it carries within it seeds of its own destruction. That's why the Bible says, "What a person sows, that he will harvest as well" (Gal. 6:7).

Many of the Corinthians had discovered that half-sex does not satisfy. It soon reaches a point of diminishing returns. Rather than producing a life of happiness they had learned the hard way that it caused frustration, broken homes, and moral deterioration. They were sick of it, but they didn't know what to do about it. They realized that it was dragging them down, but they had no power over it. Even before the Gospel of Christ had come to Corinth, many of the Corinthians had begun to scout around for a better kind of life. They were now ready to listen to someone like the Apostle Paul.

Some of these seekers had discovered the small Jewish community in Corinth. Of all the conditions that God had created in Corinth for the reception of the Gospel, this Jewish or synagogue community was the most significant. Here was the fertile soil where the seeds of the Gospel could be expected to produce a harvest thirty-, sixty-, and one hundredfold. Three kinds of people made up the synagogue community: Jews, proselytes and God-fearers.

The hard-core Jews could trace their genealogy back to Abraham, and they were proud of it. True, they were Jews of the Diaspora who had left Palestine and who had inevitably taken on some of the characteristics of the Hellenistic civilization in which they lived. But, like orthodox Jews all over the world today, they jealously guarded the traditions of their ancestors, and adhered to the law of the Old Testament. Most (but not all of them) were self-satisfied, proud, and not particularly ready to believe that Jesus Christ was the Messiah they supposedly were looking for. Of the three kinds of people in the synagogue community, they were the least responsive to the Gospel. In spite of the fact that they lived in a young city, they formed a sealed-off community and intentionally preserved their ancient customs and ideas.

The second kind of people in the synagogue were the "proselytes." They are mentioned, for example, as part of the crowd in Jerusalem on Pentecost in Acts 2. In the list of all the nationalities that heard the apostles speak in their own dialects, Luke mentions "visitors from Rome, both Jews and proselytes" (Acts 2:10). When Paul and Barnabas preached in Antioch in Pisidia, those who followed them are identified as "Jews and devout proselytes" (Acts 13:43).

Many of these proselytes were undoubtedly the sin-sick Corinthians we have been describing. They were attracted to Judaism because they found there a solution to their frustrations. The monotheism of the Jewish religion was much more satisfying to them than the confusion of gods in the pagan temples. No other religion in the world at that time offered the exalted doctrine of one omnipotent God who had created the world, who could not be represented by a man-made image, and who expected man, created in His image, to obey his moral law. Even more than that, the high moral standards of the Jews, especially the seventh commandment, did away with half-sex. Breaking with the Gentile culture they had been raised in and identifying themselves completely with the Jewish community or sub-culture, drew them into the type of disciplined ethical life that would give them inner conviction and spiritual resources to resist the temptations that constantly lured them. Furthermore, if one did happen to fall into sin, Judaism offered the rites that would cleanse them from the contamination.

To the proselytes, the sum total of these advantages of Judaism was enough to overcome the natural resistance they had to the one symbolic rite that was required for full membership in the synagogue — circumcision. While none of those who were born Jews could remember the pain of the surgery when they were only eight days old, it was a different matter for an adult man to volunteer for the ordeal. This is undoubtedly one of the principal reasons why history tells us that there were more women than men proselytes. When a man decided to become a proselyte, circumcision was the final proof of his deep conviction that the

Jewish religion was absolutely true, and that he wanted to identify himself with it as fully as he could.

While many of the proselytes were ready to accept the Gospel when they heard it, an even more fertile soil was made up of the third class of synagogue people, the God-fearers. For every pagan who submitted to circumcision, there were many more who believed in Jehovah, practiced the Jewish ethic, worshiped in the synagogue, and studied the Old Testament, but who were not convinced as to the need of undergoing circumcision, abstaining from pork, obeying the Sabbath taboos, or identifying completely with the Jewish nationalistic pride. Among the better-known God-fearers were Cornelius, the Roman centurion (Acts 10:22), and Lydia, the seller of purple in Philippi (Acts 16:14). Both accepted Christianity at the first opportunity.

Not only had the Holy Spirit prepared the soil of Corinth, especially in the synagogue community, but He had also prepared the man He had chosen to evangelize the city. In every way Paul was the proper man to enter the Jewish community in Corinth and announce the good news of salvation in Christ in terms they could all understand. Not only could Paul trace his ancestry back to Abraham with the best of them, but he also had studied under the most famous of the rabbis, Gamaliel. This was equivalent to a Ph. D. from Harvard. Having been a member of the Sanhedrin gave him an additional status among Jews which could compare today with that of a U.S. senator. Furthermore he enjoyed the coveted privilege of being a Roman citizen.

But Paul, Jewish as he was, had not been raised in Palestine. His home town, Tarsus, was a Hellenistic city in Cilicia. Undoubtedly, his family was associated with a synagogue community similar in its structure to that of Corinth. Paul, therefore, would probably have felt more at home in Corinth, for example, than he would have felt in Jerusalem where the Jews lived more of a ghetto-like life. He knew the language of the people, he knew how to act in any given situation, he understood the attitudes of the community. There were no serious cultural barriers to communication — a considerable advantage, incidentally, over most of today's missionaries.

Unlike Peter, a Palestinian Jew, Paul had found it relatively easy to throw off the trappings of Jewish legalism when he was converted. As he forcefully and successfully argued in the Jerusalem Council (Acts 15), circumcision was not to be a prerequisite for Christianity. In one of Scripture's best-known heavyweight fights, Paul faced Peter with his inconsistent behavior at Antioch (Gal. 2:11-14). In spite of his dramatic vision of the great sheet filled with unclean animals (Acts 10), and his presence in the Jerusalem Council, Peter still tended to be so legalistic that he compelled "Gentiles to live like Jews" (Gal. 2:14). Paul, who didn't have this problem, finally had to reprimand him to his face.

This broad-minded attitude concerning the details of Jewish law put Paul squarely on the wave length of the large number of God-fearers who had gathered around the synagogue community in Corinth. No wonder that from this group came the majority of Paul's converts.

Paul was a second-term missionary when he went to Corinth. He had accumulated a good deal of missionary experience on his first term, then had gone back to his home church of Antioch for his furlough. While there, he reported to his church (Acts 14:27), participated in the Jerusalem Council (Acts 15), ministered in the Antioch church (15:35), and made preparations for his second term (15:36-40). During his furlough he had undoubtedly given a great deal of thought, under the guidance of the Holy Spirit, to the strategy he would employ on his next term. As we read of his subsequent missionary work, the broad outlines of his strategy become clear.

The objective of Paul's missionary work was to plant Christian churches. In order to do this, the seed had to be sown, a harvest produced, and the fruit reaped and gathered into churches. Paul's strategy was not "broadcast sowing" on every kind of soil. In the first century, as today, Asia Minor and Europe contained many different kinds of people. Some had been prepared by the Holy Spirit to receive the Gospel, some had not. Some were, in the terms of the parable, "good soil," and some were "along the road" or "rocky soil" (Matt. 13:3-8). Paul had little time for unfertile soil. He did not commit the error of planning his strategy according to the "need" as many do today. "Need" neutralizes selective seed-sowing because all men lost and without Christ have equal need. But not all are equally receptive to the Gospel.

Paul knew beforehand that the synagogue communities were the most responsive people to the Gospel in the area he was sent to evangelize. Therefore, when he pushed out into new territory, he chose the places that had strong synagogue communities such as Thessalonica (Acts 17:1), Berea (17:10), Corinth (18:1), and Ephesus (18:19). Philippi had a functional substitute, "where we supposed that there was a place of worship" (16:13), but Paul needed a special vision to send him there (16:9). In each of these places a strong Christian church was planted.

Where there was no strong synagogue community, Paul simply passed the place by. We know of no such communities, for example, in Amphipolis and Apollonia (17:1), so Paul did not stop there. The people there had the same "need" for Christ that they had in Thessalonica, but Paul would probably have wasted precious time if he had tried to plant churches there.

One place where Paul departed from his predetermined strategy makes an interesting study. This was Athens, the great philosophical center of the ancient world. Whereas he did go into the synagogue (17:17), he also was so disturbed by the idolatry of the city that he accepted the challenge of the philosophers to meet them on their own ground, the market place and finally the Areopagus. The Athenian philosophical fraternity was obviously not fertile ground, for Paul did not see the results of his preaching there that he did in other places. While converts like Dionysius cause rejoicing (17:34) the harvest in Athens was sparce compared to Thessalonica (17:4) and Berea (17:12) where phrases such as "a large group," and "a number" are used.

As Paul continued into Corinth for his evangelistic effort he was at a seeming disadvantage in comparison to evangelistic campaigns today. No advance team had moved into Corinth to prepare the way for him, no great stadium had been rented, and, as a matter of fact, he had left the other members of his own team, Timothy and Silas, in Macedonia. They were to join him later.

Instead of holding a press conference or sending up a "gospel blimp," Paul quietly settled down in the Corinthian synagogue community and identified with them economically. In common with most Jewish teachers of the law, Paul had a trade, so he was able to move in with the Jewish family of Aquila and Priscilla and help in their cottage industry, a small tent factory (Acts 18:2, 3). Although Luke's account does not mention it, one would suspect that Paul had known of Aquila and Priscilla through mutual friends or relatives in some of the other synagogue communities he had visited previously. He may even have carried letters of introduction.

Naturally, Paul began to attend the synagogue on Saturdays. Soon he was invited to preach. His message caused a reaction and divided the members of the synagogue. It was a pattern that had occurred before, so Paul must have been prepared for it. At first the hard-core Jews might not have realized that Paul's message was so revolutionary. He used a gradual approach to gain the confidence of the greatest number before he moved on to the controversial issues which he knew would divide his listeners and cause them to take sides. Finally, when Silas and Timothy joined him and would be able to help in the follow up, Paul began "urging upon the Jews that Jesus was the Messiah" (18:5).

As Paul developed the message of Christianity, he brought out the fact that circumcision was not necessary for salvation, and that many of the other Old Testament laws did not need to be kept literally. His attack on the Jewish legalistic system caused the opposition of the Jews to break out in the open as it had done in Thessalonica and Berea. They expelled Paul from the synagogue, but it was too late. The Gospel had already taken root in many hearts, and this newly-formed Christian congregation began services in the house next door to the synagogue where a believer named Justus lived. The furious Jews might have succeeded in running Paul out of town as they had in other places if it weren't for the dramatic conversion of Crispus, the leader of the synagogue (18:8). Then when the man who apparently was his successor, Sosthenes (18:17), was converted (since his name appears with that of Paul in I Cor. 1:1), the Jewish opposition was effectively broken.

The proselytes and God-fearers were the most receptive to the Gospel, as was to have been expected. That is why Paul declares, "From now on I am going to the Gentiles" (Acts 18:6). By Gentiles he meant those who were not descendants of Abraham, and by this he did not exclude proselytes and God-fearers. Titus Justus, whose house became the first Christian church building in Corinth was a God-fearer, for example (18:7).

The reason that the Gospel of Christ was so appealing to the God-fearers and proselytes was that it carried all the advantages of Judaism without the excess baggage of the Jewish law. It maintained the high-level monotheism and the pure moral standards that these fugitives from a sex-saturated society were seeking. But such conditions as circumcision and abstention from pork were placed to one side. You did not need to become a Jew in order to be accepted by God. Furthermore, Paul's doctrine of the internal presence of the Holy Spirit, the third person of the Trinity, added a dimension of power over temptation and sin that had been absent from Judaism. Little wonder that the Christian message found a warm response among many of these Corinthian people.

The seed had been planted on fertile ground and the harvest came abundantly. The foundation had been laid for a permanent Christian church, and Paul remained in Corinth for a year and a half in follow-up work. The church was undoubtedly growing steadily all that time, and when it came time for Paul to leave, the Corinthian church might have been the largest of the younger churches.

When Paul left for Ephesus, he realized that the believers in Corinth had not reached perfection — who ever does?

But Paul was faced with the decision which every missionary must make at some time. Undoubtedly it is a missionary's most difficult decision, and for that reason it is too often postponed unreasonably. Before God, Paul came to the conclusion that the Corinthian believers had matured enough to carry on without his apostolic guidance. It was time to turn the work over to the nationals. He commended them to God, and moved on.

But had Paul left too soon? Subsequent developments in the church make this a pertinent question.

Study Questions

1. Illicit sex was one of the great social problems in the city of Corinth. Discuss how the so-called "Playboy philosophy" can affect people today, and influence the way they receive the witness to Jesus Christ. Does it harden some? Does it make some more responsive?

2. Does the United States have any communities or groups of people today that show an unusual openness to the Gospel as did the synagogue community of Corinth? Make a list of several such kinds of people. You can get a clue if you find places where churches are growing.

3. God provided Paul with special preparation for communicating the Gospel to the first-century synagogue communities. Describe some of the characteristics a person ideally should have to reach each of the contemporary groups you listed in question two.

4. Did you catch the contrast between "broadcast sowing" and establishing churches? If not, go back over page 25f. Then name some evangelistic efforts you know of today which seem to be satisfied with "broadcast sowing" rather than the more demanding task of making disciples and establishing new churches.

2

When the Cat's Away...

I Corinthians 1:1-7

AS ALL MISSIONARIES KNOW, staying too long with a newly-established church is often more dangerous than not staying long enough. Persecution had driven Paul from the two churches he established in Thessalonica and Berea shortly before reaching Corinth. He had no choice but to leave the believers on their own, probably much sooner than he would have otherwise, if the decision had been left up to him. We don't know much about the subsequent development of the Berean church, but Paul's first letter to the Thessalonians, written, incidentally, from Corinth, shows that the believers had formed a model congregation, they had grown spiritually, and were aggressively evangelistic (I Thess. 1:7, 8).

Although we must grant that no one has a final answer to this, it does seem that Paul stayed in Corinth too long. During the year and a half he was there the Corinthians had become dependent on the missionary. Without wanting to be, Paul was undoubtedly paternalistic in his relationship to the church. There probably wasn't much debate or discussion in the church as long as he was there. Whether a doctrinal issue or a moral problem, Paul's word was final and definite. This was a comfortable situation for the church, but it did not help the Christian maturity of the believers there. No one realized just how spiritually stunted the church was until Paul left.

The reference to the proverb, "When the cat's away, the mice will play," may sound somewhat irreverent, but it helps to dramatize the situation in Corinth. It may help us also to understand that twentieth-century missionaries have a lesson to learn at this point. Missionary paternalism has never helped a young church. Paul was fortunate that he did not become involved in the economic aspect of paternalism as do many of our missionaries today. He made tents so as not to be an economic burden to the church, thus avoiding the pitfall of making the church economically dependent on the missionary. A good deal of the paternalism on the mission fields today is economic, and the national church has become dependent on foreign funds. Most missionaries are aware of this, but they are finding that getting out of their situation is not an easy matter.

The devil is alert to capitalize on missionary misjudgment, and apparently, he was fully prepared to take advantage of Paul's leaving the Corinthian church. Within just a few months, the new congregation was floundering through a mass of thorny problems.

Paul's first letter to the Corinthians has disappeared. He makes clear reference to it in First Corinthians 5:9 when he says, "I wrote you in that letter not to associate with sexually immoral people." This was a predictable topic for a church made up of converted Corinthians, and undoubtedly some church member had gone back to his old ways. Since we don't have the letter, it is difficult to guess what the details were. But in any case, it was the first sign of trouble in Corinth.

What we call First Corinthians was really Paul's second letter to the church. From the letter itself we can extract enough information to reconstruct with some accuracy the events which led up to it.

Paul was in Ephesus when he wrote First Corinthians. He had gone to Ephesus right after leaving Corinth (Acts 18:19), but only for a brief visit and some preaching in the synagogue. He had taken Aquila and Priscilla, his hosts and fellow tent-makers in Corinth, and left them in Ephesus apparently for evangelistic work. Paul went on to Jerusalem, then visited his home church at Antioch. To be contemporary, we might be justified in calling this his second furlough, since he spent "some time there" (Acts 18:23). He then left on his third term, visited the churches in Galatia and Phrygia, and finally arrived back in Ephesus.

While Paul had been gone, Apollos of Alexandria had entered the scene and spent some time in Ephesus. He had plenty of enthusiasm in preaching, but knew little doctrine. Aquila and Priscilla took him under their wing, trained him as much as they could, and by the time he continued his journey the brethren in Ephesus were ready to give him a recommendation (Acts 18:27). He apparently had become quite a popular preacher. By the time Paul returned to Ephesus, Apollos had arrived in Corinth (Acts 19:1).

Whether Apollos soothed or aggravated the problems in the Corinthian church after he arrived is not known. His experience there, however, was undoubtedly much like that of any missionary who moves in to minister where others have been before. In order to put the new missionary on the defensive, the predecessor, no matter who he might have been, gets a sort of a halo painted around his head. Then those who had run into problems with the former missionary begin to come out of hiding and side up to the new missionary, tell him their grievances and try to capture his sympathy. This problem is partially reflected in the problem of divisions in the church which comes up in the next chapter.

It must have been after Apollos arrived and settled down in Corinth that "the Chloe family" (I Cor. 1:11) made a trip from Corinth to Ephesus and told Paul something of what was going on back home. Not much is known about Chloe for certain, but she may well have been the owner of a commercial firm called "House of Chloe," and the individuals who saw Paul in Ephesus might have been some of her employees or slaves on a buying trip. Chances are that she was a member of the Corinthian church, although we have no proof of this except for the fact that she must have been well known to the believers there since Paul made reference to her without any explanation.

The firsthand news that they brought from Corinth included the report of divisions in the church. They must have been well informed, since Paul's discussion of the problem in chapters 1-4 is based on accurate detail. These same people might also have told Paul about the problem of immorality dealt with in chapters 5 and 6, although this is simply a conjecture.

Paul was sufficiently concerned with this bad news that he decided to send one of his best fellow-workers, Timothy, to handle the problem. Timothy undoubtedly was traveling north around the Aegean Sea, passing through Philippi and Thessalonica on the way. The young minister had not yet arrived in Corinth when some more developments took place.

Some of the brethren in Corinth had become so disturbed about the troubles in the church that they decided to write Paul a letter and explain the situation to him. One of the things they wrote about was the dispute concerning marriage which comes up in chapter 7. Paul begins this chapter by saying, "Concerning the subjects of your correspondence. . . ." Apparently three members of the church, Stephanas, Fortunatus, and Achaicus (I Cor. 16:17), were the ones who brought the letter to Paul. They undoubtedly also filled him in on many details that were not covered in the letter.

This was not all. By this time Apollos had returned from Corinth to Ephesus and was with Paul (I Cor. 16:12). He also would have given Paul his viewpoint as to the events in Corinth.

After getting all this information, Paul began to realize that the troubles were more serious than he had thought at first. He then became a little nervous about having sent Timothy. Timothy was a good man, but perhaps a little young and immature to handle the complex situation there in Corinth. "See to it that his [Timothy's] presence with you is free from embarrassment . . . let no one slight him . . . ," Paul writes to the Corinthians (I Cor. 16:10, 11).

There was no time to waste, so Paul decided to compose a

long letter to the Corinthians. No one rejoices when sin enters a church, but nevertheless God used the murky Corinthian situation to bring a permanent blessing to future gener-
ations of Christians through Paul's epistle. Not one of the
troubles in Corinth was essentially different from the troubles which plague many of our churches today. Paul's frank
discussions of what was going on there ring a strikingly contemporary note. He tells it like it is. First Corinthians has
more practical advice for Christians than any other book in
the Bible. That's why it's a book that can turn your church
on today, even though it was written twenty centuries ago.

Paul joins Sosthenes' name to his own as he begins to
write (1:1). This does not mean that Sosthenes was a co-
author, since Paul uses the first person singular all the way
through, and closes with "Here is my greeting in my own
handwriting" (16:21). But Paul was being tactful when he
associated publicly with the name of one of the outstanding
converts of Corinth, who apparently was in Ephesus with
Paul at the time of writing. He also includes his title of
"apostle," as is his custom in most of his epistles.

The Corinthian church clearly was not to be the only
beneficiary of the truths of the letter, even in the mind of
Paul as he wrote. Whereas he addresses it to "the church of
God at Corinth" (1:2), he also adds that it is for "all who in
every place invoke the name of our Lord Jesus Christ."
From the beginning it was written for your church and mine.

Eight major problems had invaded the Corinthian church.
The best way to study First Corinthians is not chapter by
chapter, but rather problem by problem. Each one of the
problems has its own built-in outline, as Charles Woodbridge
has pointed out. He once said that First Corinthians is a
"3-D epistle," since each section contains a *difficulty,* a *doctrine,* and a *decision.* I have not been able to improve on
this method of analysis, so after admitting that it is a pedagogical rather than an exegetical outline, I have decided to
follow through with it.

By the *difficulty* we mean the precise problem in the Corinthian church that needed to be dealt with. Some of these

difficulties are set forth in great detail in the epistle itself such as the divisions (chapters 1-4), the open fornication (chapters 5 and 6), and the abuse of the Lord's table (chapter 11). Some need to be extracted from the general tenor of the passage such as the marriage problems (chapter 7), and the use of spiritual gifts (chapters 12-14). Others need a separate historical reconstruction such as the matter of eating meat offered to idols (chapters 8-10). Most of the difficulties involve ethics rather than theology, but the matter of the resurrection (chapter 15) is strictly theological.

In each case Paul deals with, he develops a particular *doctrine* which will undergird what he has to say about the issue. This involves the eternal principles which must be applied to any similar difficulty in any church. In other words, if we accurately identify these principles, they will be just as binding on twentieth-century churches as they were on first-century churches.

This is not always true when we come to the *decision*. Often the decision that Paul made in his recommendations to the church in Corinth was conditioned by certain historical or cultural factors which are not exactly the same today. Precisely in their failure to understand this important principle of interpretation some believers have not grasped just what the Holy Spirit is trying to say to our churches through First Corinthians. This does not mean that the *doctrine* has changed, but it does mean that the same doctrine can be applied to one cultural situation in a certain way and to another cultural situation in another way. A literal transplant of some of Paul's decisions makes little sense to us today. Admittedly, it is a delicate task to attempt to apply this rule in each case, but the potential results are well worth the effort. From time to time throughout the book this will come up. One of the most obvious applications concerns the wearing of veils in church services (chapter 11). Most women find it difficult to apply this today, but in their questioning of Paul's decision, they should be careful not to reject at the same time Paul's doctrine, which is just as valid today as it ever was.

More on this later, but before moving on to begin our analysis of First Corinthians problem by problem, it would be well to attempt to locate the one underlying difficulty in the church in general. The basic problem of the Corinthians is again a contemporary problem, for many of our churches are struggling with it today. In a capsule, it is this: how much difference should there be between the church and the world? Or to come at it from the other direction: how closely should the church identify herself with the world?

Dietrich Bonhoeffer, one of the most influential of the modern theologians even after his death, proposed that we should develop a "religionless Christianity," and concentrate on moving the church into the world. To the degree that the church succeeds in identifying herself with the world, say Bonhoeffer and his followers, she is fulfilling the prophetic mission which God has given her. Christian theologians should really know better than this. The Christians at Corinth tried it and lost out. We should listen more closely to history's lessons. On what grounds could we expect to do what the Corinthians did and come out any better?

The Corinthians, like most Greeks, loved worldly wisdom and had a tendency to group themselves around the popular philosopher of the day. For them it was almost a sport — they would root for a philosopher much like we root for a baseball team. This worldly practice found its way into the church, and teams began to line up behind their favorite theologians, causing dissensions and rivalry.

Not only worldly philosophy, but also worldly ethical standards began to work their way into the church. It was a giant step from what we have called the sex-saturated society to Christian purity. Therefore, instead of maintaining a definite separation from the morals of the world around them, the Corinthians chuckled quietly when they found that one of the church members was living in incest. Again and again, for not taking a clean-cut stand of separation from the world, the Corinthian Christians became involved in such things as idolatry, drunkenness, and false doctrine. The root of the evil in the Corinthian church, then, involved an erroneous view of the relationship of the church to the world. In summary, instead of the church's winning the world as it should have been doing, the world was rapidly winning the Corinthian church. The devil was employing a subtle and effective technique to destroy all that the Apostle Paul had accomplished in Corinth. Paul, happily, recognized the danger and wrote his letter in time to put a halt to the trend.

Identification with the world was called "carnality" by Paul in those days, and it should be recognized as carnality today also. The world will never be won by worldly Christians — it will be won by Christians who have made a break with the world, but who at the same time love the world with an evangelistic passion. This basic truth underlies all parts of First Corinthians, and we must keep it in mind as we move into a consideration of the specific problems.

Study Questions

1. Define what was meant in the chapter by "difficulty, doctrine and decision." An example was given of one of Paul's decisions which would not necessarily apply today (the veil). Do you agree that it is possible that a particular doctrine could produce one decision in the first century, but a different one in the twentieth?

2. Think of some other "doctrines" which might lead to different "decisions" depending on the circumstances. (These examples do not have to come from First Corinthians.) Take, for example, the commandment, "honor thy father and thy mother."

3. Does the answer to the above questions mean that Christian ethics are relative and not absolute? Think this one through carefully.

4. Pinpoint some specific instances of how the world has affected your church or churches you know about. Which of these would you consider most dangerous for the future of the church? How would you deal with them?

5. If you don't identify or associate somewhat with the world, you can never communicate with people there and win them to Christ. Where do you draw the line between identification and separation?

3

Carnality Splits Churches

1 Corinthians 1-4

LIVING IN WHAT CHURCH HISTORIANS may eventually call "The Ecumenical Century" brings us all face to face with the problems involved in unity and divisions in the church. In this first large section of First Corinthians, chapters 1-4, Paul analyzes a church-splitting situation and lays down some guidelines for dealing with it.

It is well to recognize at the outset that there is nothing wrong with either disagreements or diversity in the church. Since we're human beings, disagreements are inevitable. Few of us see things from exactly the same point of view, and naturally we often arrive at divergent conclusions on matters. Diversity among Christians is something that God Himself produces, as we shall see in detail in chapter 8. But neither disagreement nor diversity should lead to division.

Paul says in 1:10, "I beg of you, brothers, that all of you agree, that you eliminate factions among you." The situation in Corinth had gone too far. The church was splitting into weak and mutually antagonistic fragments. In verse 11, Paul speaks of their contentions. This is the same word which appears as "strife" in the list of the works of the flesh in Galatians 5:20. By using the word, Paul puts his finger on the real source of the trouble — carnality. The works of the flesh were overshadowing the fruit of the Spirit in Corinth.

DIFFICULTY

Philosophy was a great sport for the ancient Greeks. Although philosophy in Corinth might have been minor league in comparison to Athens, it was important enough to get excited about. In the days before newspapers, motion pictures and television, large crowds would gather to listen to some teacher or other expound different aspects of his particular world view. The best of the philosophers were able to draw circles of faithful followers to themselves, commanding the same type of loyalty that we see in baseball fans today. Many had identified themselves so closely with their teacher that they were willing to argue or even to fight for his prestige.

We have already pointed out that the basic problem in the Corinthian church was that the world was gradually winning the church rather than the church winning the world. Their divisions illustrate this perfectly. Out in the world they enjoyed forming philosophical parties and arguing with each other. They carried this attitude over to the church, where they formed four religious parties. Each party chose the name of a prominent Christian leader as its rallying point (1:12).

First came the *Paul Party*. Paul's name predictably would be one of the first chosen since he was the founder of the church. We don't have exact information as to the details of the ideas that the members of any of these groups had in common, but assuming that the names they chose had some correlation with their ideas, it is not difficult to conjecture and attempt to reconstruct the situation. One of the amazing aspects of doing so is to realize that things haven't changed so much in twenty centuries. In many of our churches today we find Christians who might have belonged to one party or the other in Corinth. Happily, in most cases they are able to get along with each other. This is the way it should be. The Corinthians, however, didn't know how to handle the differences among themselves.

The Paul Party was probably made up of the circle of

first converts, many of whom might have been led to the Lord by Paul himself. This was a source of personal pride for them, as if they were a little more securely saved because Paul had been involved. Whenever an argument would arise, they would claim an inside track on the proper interpretation of Paul's teaching. They were probably reluctant to change anything that had been done while Paul had been in Corinth. They were traditionalists to the bone and probably kept referring to "the good old days." They had fallen into the trap of reasoning that because God never changes, the world in which we live or the circumstances under which we work never change either. Their tendency was to deify the status quo.

Ironically, by forming a Paul Party the group failed to obey the clear teaching of the leader whose name they had chosen. This often happens. I recall that when Karl Barth was in the United States he commented that he found it impossible to recognize the theology of many "Barthians." Paul himself must have had some premonition that this would happen when he was still in Corinth. According to 1:13-17, he did his best to avoid having his person too intimately connected with any of the believers. He says, "I am thankful to have baptized none of you except Crispus and Gaius, so that none of you may claim baptism in my name." Possibly without fully realizing it, this group was dishonoring the apostle Paul. As the letter shows, he deeply regretted his name being associated with any faction.

Others had grouped themselves in the *Apollos Party*. Apollos, as we have seen, went to Corinth to minister after Paul had left. A converted Alexandrian Jew, he became famous in the early church as an eloquent preacher and a skillful apologist (Acts 18:24). There was no difference between Paul and Apollos as far as the fundamental truths of Christianity are concerned, so we are not dealing with some false sect that was beginning to be formed in Corinth. It is true that Apollos was doctrinally confused when he first arrived in Ephesus, but after Paul's companions, Aquila and

Priscilla, straightened him out (Acts 18:26), he had no problem with false doctrine.

Chances are that he did have another characteristic, however. He was born and brought up in the city of Alexandria. This city historically was the center of what is known as the allegorical method of interpretation of the Scriptures. Apollos, perhaps even before his conversion, had undoubtedly been in contact with Philo of Alexandria, a Jewish leader there who developed an elaborate allegorical interpretation of the Old Testament in an attempt to relate Judaism to Hellenistic philosophy. The Christian Church at Alexandria absorbed this trend, later manifested in such well-known church fathers as Clement and Origen.

While Apollos would have repudiated the Gnostic-like doctrine of Philo, his background would have undoubtedly left him with a liberal attitude toward many of the fine points of Christianity. He would not have shared the views of what we call liberalism or modernism today, but in regard to many of the secondary issues of Christianity where legitimate differences of opinion can arise, he would have tended toward flexibility rather than hair-splitting. His name was used, therefore, by those Corinthian believers who looked upon themselves as sharing a similar open-minded point of view.

Most directly opposed to them would be the *Cephas Party*. They perhaps went to an extreme of legalistic and Pharisaical interpretation of Christian life and doctrine. They adopted Peter's name (it was Cephas in Aramaic) because he had an image of strictness, especially concerning the Jewish law. Peter had never visited Corinth, but his name was well-known in Christian circles. Perhaps Paul had told them of his argument with Peter in Antioch when he had to reprimand Peter to his face for not taking a stand against the Judaizers (Gal. 2:11-14). Not only did this group in Corinth feel inclined to take Peter's side on this, but the name of the leader of the original twelve apostles added to the status of their party, at least according to their worldly reasoning.

It bears repeating that, as far as we know, no major

Christian doctrine was at stake here. The Cephas Party was not heretical, or Paul undoubtedly would have said something about it. They simply had strong feelings on details of belief and behavior, much more strict than those of the Apollos Party, for example. Our churches today have the same type of person. Instead of saying "don't eat with Gentiles" they set forth a more up-to-date list of "don'ts" and usually their Christian ethic revolves around negativisms. Donald Grey Barnhouse used to caricature them as those who say, "I don't smoke, I don't chew, and I don't go with girls who do!"

Now the last party had chosen the best name, but manifested what was perhaps the worst attitude. By calling itself the *Christ Party,* its members betrayed a subtle spiritual pride, suggesting that they considered themselves the only true Christians. They were the exclusivists. They felt they had a corner on the truth. They probably harbored grave doubts as to the salvation of those who did not agree with them. And if some of the others might have been saved, they were considered second-class citizens of the Kingdom of God.

The Christ Party made the mistake that some make today of not admitting the possibility that they could have been wrong. They would not have been at all aware that they were participating just as much in the Corinthian carnality than their brethren in the other three parties. This type of Christian often arrives at an I've-got-God-on-a-leash mentality.

The total effect of the four parties in the church was a serious church split. It must be repeated that underlying this four-way split were wrong attitudes rather than wrong doctrines. In a word the problems were due to what the Bible calls carnality. Paul was disturbed with them. "You are still unspiritual (carnal)," he writes. "Insofar as you entertain jealousy and contentiousness, are you not unspiritual (carnal), and do you not behave like the unconverted?" (3:3). Their lives should have been sufficiently transformed by the Gospel that they could be distinguished from the people of the world who reveled in dissension, argument, debate, and law suits.

The distinction between attitude and doctrine is a key one. A church or a group of Christians who takes a stand against heresy is not carnal, even if a church split results (Titus 3:10). The Bible clearly teaches that heresy must not be tolerated in the Church. Heresy, however, can arise only when essential Christian doctrines are at stake. The type of secondary issues and proud attitudes that had infected the Corinthians were bad, but not in the category of heresy. The difficulty comes in that most of us have a hard time at knowing exactly where to draw the line between what is essential and what is secondary. On many borderline cases there is no final answer at all. Sensitive Christians will always find themselves living in a tension in this gray area.

The Corinthians were not in the gray area, however. They had split their church on clearly secondary matters. Heresy was indeed present in the Corinthian church. Their view of the doctrine of the Resurrection was badly twisted, and Paul deals with this in great detail in chapter 15. But apparently that doctrinal problem was an across-the-board heresy, entering to some extent into all of the four parties, and not itself the cause of the church split.

DOCTRINE

In laying the doctrinal foundation for his recommendation to the Corinthians, Paul begins with the concept of "wisdom," the famous *sophia* that the Greeks in general sought after in their philosophical societies. In this doctrinal passage (1:18—2:16), Paul condemns the wisdom of the world at the same time drawing a contrast between that and the true wisdom of God.

The false wisdom which plagued the Corinthians was evident not only in the secular world around them (1:18-25), but unfortunately also in the church itself (1:26-31). The Greeks frequently determined status by intellectual attainment, measured by the academic titles and honors that the world bestowed upon the erudite and the eloquent. Their tendency was to treat Christianity as just one more philosophy, joining the others in the endless search for *sophia*. Paul, however, refused to allow Christianity to be lowered to the level that the world had established, "that your faith might not rest on human wisdom but on divine strength" (2:5). Since the Christian faith comes as a revelation from the sovereign God, it cannot offer itself as a subject of debate on the grounds of human wisdom.

The conflict between secular wisdom and the true wisdom of God would not have been so bad taken by itself, if the attitude of the secular philosophers had not crept into the church. The believers were holding their own particular interpretations with such a spirit of worldly arrogance that divisions in the church were inevitable. They mistakenly thought that as Christians they were supposed to defend Christianity with the power of human reason, a danger which can eventually destroy all possibility of intellectual humility. They never framed their ideas as opinions — they were all *convictions!* Then, as now, such an attitude produced a cultic Christianity. Cultic mentality allows no room for disagreement or debate. Result: "I belong to Paul; I belong to Apollos. . . ."

Paul uses the same word for wisdom, *sophia,* when he goes on to speak of the wisdom of God (2:6-13). In applying this true wisdom to practical life, there is a part to be played by the believer himself (2:6-9) and a part to be played by the Holy Spirit (2:10-13). In all cases, the believer must recognize that true wisdom begins with God's revelation, never with human efforts to arrive at the truth (2:9).

This is a difficult thing to admit for one who has always prided himself on his own intellectual powers. A worldly philosopher does not usually like to admit the existence of mysteries which he never could discover by his own efforts at contemplation. But when the believer does recognize that "we give expression to divine wisdom in the form of a mystery" (2:7), and that God's revelation is prior to all human wisdom, he thereby confesses his own finitude, and acquires a measure of intellectual humility. For the first time he comes to the place where he is able to say, "This is what I believe, *but I may be wrong.*" With this attitude as to the secondary aspects of the Christian faith, church splits are not likely to occur.

Once the believer submits to the authority of divine revelation, the Holy Spirit takes it upon Himself to provide the illumination necessary to understand it. "Of these matters we speak, not in words taught by human wisdom, but in words taught by the Spirit" (2:13), Paul says. This was language that the Corinthians understood well. Their *sophia* was to come from the Spirit of God.

One thing that could and did stand in the way of the communication of knowledge by the Holy Spirit was carnality. While it might be expected that the "natural man" (2:14, KJV) would not be able to receive the special wisdom of the Spirit of God since he has not acquired that spiritual wave length which only the new birth produces, Paul explains to the Corinthians that the carnal Christian is little better as far as his understanding of spiritual truth is concerned. A carnal Christian must be fed with "milk" and not with "solid food" (3:2), so therefore he will not find the *sophia* of the Holy Spirit that he could have if he were a spiritual Christian. Spirituality would have given the Corinthians both *sophia* and also the solution to their problem of divisions. This *sophia* comes not through further academic training or even through more doctrinal teaching, but rather through deeper sanctification, a closer walk with Jesus Christ.

DECISION

Having described the *difficulty* through which the Corinthians were passing and the *doctrine* Paul expounded as a foundation for the solution, we can move on to the conclusion, or the *decision.* Paul's decision (3:5—4:21) involves three suggestions for the Corinthian believers:

1. *Strive for wider cooperation among Christians* (3:5-9). Paul and Apollos worked together and were of one

mind. Paul, who sowed the seed in Corinth, was happy to have Apollos water it (3:6). Both rejoiced together when God gave the increase, or church growth. To them it was absurd that the Corinthians would organize parties around their names as a basis for splitting the church. If they followed the example of their leaders they would have worked in cooperation rather than in conflict. Paul commands the believers in Corinth that they forget about their four parties and get together.

What does this mean for us today in an ecumenical age? If we are to make a comparison, we immediately see that there are two major differences between our twentieth-century church and the church in Corinth. The first difference is that Paul faced a united church which had just begun to split. We today face a long-divided church making herculean efforts to unite. Some of the major efforts toward union today appear to be based on programs and attitudes just as carnal as those underlying the Corinthian splits. Christians should beware of carnality wherever it is operative.

The second difference is that many of today's divisions are not caused by secondary issues as were the Corinthians'. Some have arisen over what are obviously essential issues such as death-of-God theology or the new morality. Union does not involve a simple change of attitude in many cases, but rather a change of world view. This makes today's situation more complex.

Paul commanded the Corinthian believers to get together, to abandon their petty differences. The same is true today. So many of our contemporary divisions have been produced by secondary issues that we have before us a tremendous potential to dissolve them and explore new avenues of cooperation and fellowship among Christians who have given their full allegiance to Jesus Christ. In this sense Paul's decision for the Corinthians is also a decision for us.

One problem that muddies the waters is that the liberals have a tendency to make their list of what they consider secondary issues too long. They often include inspiration and authority of Scripture, the historicity of the Virgin Birth, the miracles, and the Resurrection, the necessity for individual salvation, or the Second Coming of Christ as optional doctrines. On the other hand, it must be admitted that many of the more conservative brethren go to the other extreme and tend to exaggerate the list of essentials, including at times such secondary issues as the mode of baptism, liturgy for the Lord's Supper, details of the process of sanctification, gifts of the Holy Spirit, or a particular millennial belief. Both err in that they allow the world's wisdom to govern spiritual matters, much as the Corinthians did.

Somewhere in between the extremes lies the proper ground for cooperation and fellowship. True Christians must always be willing to enter into dialogue with each other trusting the Spirit of God to lead both to a more Biblical position. We must not glibly jump on the ecumenical bandwagon, glossing over our differences as if they really weren't important. Neither can we complacently sit on our pet doctrines and wait for everyone else to recognize *our* view of the truth and join *us*.

2. Paul's second suggestion for the Corinthian believers is to *have full confidence in the work of the Holy Spirit* (3: 16, 17). Once another person is born again, he enjoys the ministry of the Holy Spirit in his heart just as we do. It is presumptuous to jump to the conclusion that any one Christian can have a corner on the Holy Spirit. God plays no favorites.

Once we admit this, however, we place ourselves in a precarious situation. Logically, if the Spirit is ministering in the life of my brother, whoever he may be, there exists at least the possibility that He may be able to lead my brother better than He is leading me. Sometimes this is hard to accept, but to do so is a sure sign of Christian maturity. If such an attitude of true humility penetrated the Church of Christ on all levels, problems of church-splitting would soon disappear.

3. Finally, Paul suggests to the Corinthians that they *stop judging their brother in Christ* (3:10-15, 18-21). The great passage on the Judgment Seat of Christ appears here to

show the Corinthians that in the final analysis each Christian is responsible before God for his own acts. Since God will judge each individual according to his works, Christians should stop taking upon themselves God's prerogative of judgment. Paul exhorts, "So do not pass premature judgment before the Lord comes" (4:5).

Once again, it must be stressed that this principle does not apply to doctrinal heresy or immoral conduct. It applies to the secondary matters of faith and practice which tragically separate true brothers in Christ.

How to handle church-splitters? Look behind whatever superficial reasons might be given and locate the carnality that certainly exists. Divisions in the church can inevitably be traced to carnal Christians who have allowed themselves to be governed more by worldly attitudes than spiritual ones. In obedience to the Word of God, when essentials are not involved, each of us today should strive to heal the divisions which exist and do our best to prevent the occurrence of new ones. This is Scriptural "ecumenism."

Study Questions

1. List some known areas of disagreement or diversity between members of your church or denomination. Is there danger that any of these could eventually cause division?

2. Classify each item in the above list as either "attitude" or "doctrine." Then think of some other matters that have or could cause problems in churches, and attempt to divide them between "secondary matters" and "essential matters."

3. Think through the implications of the phrase, "intellectual humility." If this were characteristic of more Christians today, how specifically (in cases you know about) could it help relationships among Christians?

4. Try to recall the details of some church splits you know about. Analyze each one, and then give your opinion as to whether the picture would have been different if the three subpoints under Paul's decision in this chapter had been applied.

4

When Division Helps the Church

I Corinthians 5-6

CARNALITY PLAYS FUNNY TRICKS. It often turns Christian behavior upside down. Because they were carnal, the Christians in Corinth divided when they were supposed to be united, and they remained united when they were supposed to be divided.

Is there ever a time when Christians are supposed to divide? Can division ever help a church?

The division into parties which bore the names of Paul, Apollos, Cephas and Christ was altogether wrong because it was caused by wrong attitudes over secondary matters. Neither heresy nor immorality was basically involved. Chapters 1-4 of Paul's first letter to the Corinthians show why this kind of division has no place in the Christian Church. Division over secondary matters weakens the church.

DIFFICULTY

In chapters 5 and 6, Paul faces a totally different problem. A member of the Corinthian church was living in sin with his stepmother (5:1)! Immorality of any kind cannot be considered secondary. Adultery and fornication consistently appear at the top of the major lists of sins in the New Testament. True, Corinth was Corinth — one of the fleshpots of the ancient world. But for all their sex saturation, the pagan Corinthians had certain "standards." One of them was not to commit incest. Paul says that this sin was "a kind which does not occur among the Gentiles" (5:1). Incredibly, a sin that even the pagans shunned had invaded the church!

Although incest in the church shocked Paul deeply, it was not, as far as he was concerned, the most serious trouble. In this case we have a double *difficulty*. Even worse than the sin itself was the apparent attitude of the entire congregation toward it. "And you, rather than grieving about it enough to remove the person who committed such a deed, are you still puffed up?" (5:2). The secret had leaked; it was one of those scandals that everyone was talking about!

Here is one of the funny tricks of carnality. Because of it, the believers had allowed pride to creep into their hearts over the matter. Paul labels it "boasting" in 5:6. But of what could they possibly be proud? Obviously they were not boasting that they had a case of incest. They could not be proud of the sin itself. Rather, their pride undoubtedly centered in their concept of "broad-mindedness." The elders had probably said to one another as they discussed the case: "What our good brother does in his private life is entirely his affair. His doctrine is straight. He attends church regularly. He is pleasant and friendly. He obeys the golden rule. Furthermore, this affair with his stepmother might be a meaningful relationship for both of them. Our obligation is to continue to love him. Let's not be pharisaical about the thing!"

It apparently never occurred to the Corinthian believers that they should not excuse the brother, but rather excommunicate him.

This same carnal attitude of boasting about broad-mindedness is sweeping our churches today. Many churchmen call it "situation ethics" or the "new morality." But there is nothing new under the sun. The Corinthians had experimented with the "new morality" back in the first century. Broad-mindedness may be a pleasing characteristic, but when

it is used as an excuse to condone immorality, it becomes
sub-Christian.

DOCTRINE

So much for the *difficulty* in the Corinthian (and the
contemporary) church. Paul moves on to his *doctrine* (5:
6-13; 6:9-21), or the principles underlying his final *decision*
in the case. He establishes four major principles:

1. *Immorality in the church must be treated like leaven
in the Passover feast* (5:6-8). No Jew would celebrate the
Passover with leavened bread. But Paul compares the sin in
the Corinthian church with leaven. Perhaps this man was
the only member of the whole church living in immorality;
nevertheless the whole congregation shared the guilt of his
immorality. "Celebrate the feast" in verse 8 might well be a
reference to the Lord's Supper. If so, when a congregation
allows participation in the Lord's Supper of one member who
is known to be living in sin, the whole ordinance loses its
value for the group. There is only one thing to do with the
old leaven: purge it out (5:7).

2. *Separation has a definite place in the Christian life*
(5:9-13). In dealing with the matter of separation from
sinners, Paul makes a very important distinction. There is
no reason for a Christian to separate himself from unbelievers
who are living in sin. The phrase, "then you must get out of
the world altogether" (5:10) shows that Paul was no advo-
cate of monasticism or the formation of an evangelical ghetto.
It is clearly a Christian duty to maintain contact with the
world in order to win people to Christ. No one should be
overly concerned about the sins in the life of an unconverted
friend when the matter of sin in general is his basic problem.

On the other hand, when a Christian allows fornication,
covetousness, idolatry, railing, drunkenness, or any other
scandalous sin to come into his life, the other members of
the congregation must judge him and "Expel that wicked
person from your own company" (5:13).

3. *The worldly solution is to let secular courts judge*

church matters (6:1-8). Whether we are talking about gross immorality or mild disagreements between Christians, these problems should be handled in the church, not taken before unbelieving judges. The Corinthians were looking for the easy way out of their troubles, and so as to avoid hurt feelings in the congregation, they passed the buck to the secular courts. This, of course, was a hangover from their former attraction to law suits when they were still in the world. This was wrong. Here is another case of Christians running away from their responsibility of handling church discipline with boldness when the need arises.

4. *High standards of moral purity must be maintained at all cost* (6:9-20). The difficulty started with sexual sin, and Paul ends his discussion where it began. To the Greek mentality it was strange to hear the doctrine that the body could glorify God. Their background of philosophical dualism had taught them that a man's spirit was good, but that his material body was always bad. By teaching that the physical body of a Christian is a "member of Christ" (5:15) and the "temple of the Holy Spirit" (6:19), Paul raises morality to a level that the ordinary Corinthian had not dreamed of.

It is obvious that Paul had not allowed himself to be swayed by the advocates of the "new morality." His standards were firm and high: "the body is not meant for immorality, but for the Lord." "The immoral man sins against his own body." "Shun immorality." There are no qualms here about stating Christian ethics in absolute terms.

DECISION

The upshot is that the incest in the Corinthian church had to be dealt with by the congregation itself. In Paul's *decision* he suggests not more broad-mindedness, but strict discipline. In this case the discipline consists of excommunication. Since excommunication is such a delicate matter, and rather marginal to the thinking of many Christians today, it merits careful explanation.

The verse which says, "let such a person be handed over

to Satan for the destruction of the flesh" (5:5) is one of the classic difficulties for Biblical interpretation. Without getting sidetracked on the debates over its exegesis, let's simply agree that whatever it means in detail, at least it teaches that the brother should be excluded from the fellowship of the congregation. Paul repeats the same thought in other phrases: "remove the person who committed such a deed" (5:2), "purge out the old yeast" (5:7), "you must not associate with him" (5:11), and "expel that wicked person from your own company" (5:13).

While excommunication is not a Biblical word, it is nevertheless a Biblical concept. It accurately describes what Paul is advocating here. Jesus expressed it: "treat him like a pagan and a tax gatherer" (Matt. 18:17). Although admittedly an extreme measure, excommunication is Scriptural both for the Corinthians and for us. Not to apply it when necessary reflects carnality in the church if the Corinthian situation can be taken as a valid example.

Before anyone contemplates excommunication, three prerequisites, all clearly implied in Paul's introduction to this section, must be fulfilled.

In the first place there must be no doubt that the sin is really being committed. Discipline cannot be based on rumors; it must be undergirded by solid fact. If a discipline case is based on faulty evidence, the church often suffers a serious backlash. The incest in Corinth was not just hearsay, but common knowledge (5:1), so this first prerequisite was fulfilled.

Secondly, the moral problem in question must be a recognized sin before anyone can be disciplined for it. There should be no question about fornication in anyone's mind, so again this prerequisite was fulfilled in Corinth. But when it comes to doubtful issues such as smoking, dancing, failure to tithe, the length of one's hair, Sunday observance, or other such things, each church must decide for itself where to draw the line between prohibition and permission, or whether to draw a line at all. Without a definite line, however, there can be no discipline.

Finally, sin which precipitates excommunication must be a measurable sin. Some definite sins are quite unmeasurable and therefore almost impossible to judge. If you try open discipline for such subjective things as envy, hypocrisy, bitterness, or lack of love, you are in for a difficult time. Without doubt these are some of the most destructive sins in the Church, but ordinarily they fall outside the limits of discipline. They must be left to God. We must admit that there is some difference between a man openly living with his stepmother, and one who might "look on a woman to lust after her." One is measurable, the other (unless openly confessed) is not.

Excommunication is such a severe discipline that we should regard it as absolutely a last resort. All other possibilities should be exhausted first. Prior steps are listed for us in Matthew 18:15-17. When the sin is discovered, the offender should be faced up with his fault in a private interview. If he repents, that ends the affair. If he does not, the second visit should include two or three witnesses. If this fails, the problem should then be taken to the church and handled either through the congregation or its representatives. If repentance is not then forthcoming, the brother must be excommunicated.

What does this imply? Most people consider the basic discipline as exclusion from the communion table and from the ordinary membership privileges of the church. Most agree also that the offender should not be permitted to participate in other public roles such as special musical numbers, choir, public prayer, Sunday school teaching, church committees, etc. Some go even further (and I agree with them), requesting that the disciplined brother not even attend church services until the matter is satisfactorily cleared up.

Two purposes of excommunication stand out. The first is the *correction* of the erring brother. Paul implies this in I Corinthians 5:5 where he desires "in order that the spirit may be saved on the day of the Lord Jesus," and he states it clearly in Galatians 6:1, placing the burden for "set[ting] him straight" on "you spiritual persons."

Fortunately we have a success story here. Most commentators agree that the passage in II Corinthians 2:5-8 refers to the same man who was dealt with in I Corinthians. Apparently when discipline was wisely applied and he was cut off from Christian fellowship, he repented, changed his ways, and was to be admitted once again into the church. Our primary objective in cases like this should be to heal the wound in the body of Christ.

Some churches err by fixing a time for discipline. For example, a member sins, and he is excommunicated for six months. There is no Biblical basis for setting a time as if it were a prison sentence. Discipline is not punitive. Scripturally discipline ends whenever sincere repentance appears. If the offender repents after one month, the other five are superfluous. If six months pass and he has not yet repented, he has no right to be taken off discipline. Jesus said that Christian forgiveness must be offered "seventy times seven" (Matt. 18:22). This, of course, refers only to sincere heart repentance. Hypocrisy is a fact of life, and admittedly there are cases when the sincerity of repentance can be legitimately doubted. In such cases a trial period might be recommended between the verbal repentance and the final restoration, introducing a legitimate time factor. This is most common when the same offense has been repeated. But this is quite different from the prison-sentence type of discipline.

Of course, some excommunicated people are beyond restoration. This is a sad, but true, fact of Christian life. If the disciplined brother does not repent and return to the church, it does not always mean that the discipline has failed. Correction is only one of two equally important purposes for excommunication.

The second is *protection* of the church. Official discipline protects the testimony of the church in the eyes of the community it serves (I Cor. 5:7), as well as protecting other members of the church from becoming infected with the same sin (5:6). For the sake of the public testimony of the church, many believe that the disciplined brother should not even be allowed to attend the services. The outside world must realize that the church maintains high moral and spiritual standards at all costs. If the ultimate cost is a member of a church or a whole family, it is a price which must be paid to maintain a meaningful Christian testimony.

Once again, excommunication is a Scriptural principle. Churches like the Corinthian church, which do not apply it when they should, are carnal churches. Unfortunately, there are many churches like that today. Perhaps many of us could profitably re-examine our own congregations to see if failure to follow this Biblical precept might not be one of the reasons for lack of spiritual power in these days.

Here is another place where First Corinthians may help turn your church on.

Study Questions

1. Explain in your own words the twofold difficulty described in this chapter. Which of the two do you think caused Paul more distress?

2. In your opinion, why is excommunication practiced so infrequently in Protestant churches today? Is this true of your church?

3. Make a list of problems which might arise in churches today that would be serious enough to consider excommunication.

4. What happens to a church which consistently shirks its responsibility to excommunicate members who are involved in scandalous sin or heresy?

5. When, if ever, should a time limit be placed on a member's excommunication?

5

The Pros and Cons of Celibacy

I Corinthians 7

WHEN PAUL wrote First Corinthians he was not married. This has caused Biblical scholars to raise the perplexing question: Was Paul a bachelor or a widower? Interesting arguments have been given on each side, but First Corinthians 7 does seem to be written by someone who knew by experience what marriage was all about. Discounting the unlikely possibility that Paul was separated from a living wife, it seems that he was a widower, able to write from the point of view of a person who had been single, married, and later — perhaps tragically — unmarried. Of course the Holy Spirit could have inspired him in spite of his background, but ordinarily the personality of the inspired writers was used, rather than bypassed, by the Holy Spirit.

DIFFICULTY

Once again, the notorious carnality of the Corinthian Christians produced the difficulty which this time caused Paul to write the Bible's longest and most thorough essay on marriage. Spiritual Christians are usually characterized by qualities such as "forbearance, gentleness, and self-control" as fruits of the Holy Spirit who lives within them (Gal. 5:22, 23). On the other hand, carnality will drive Christians to extremes such as "jealousy, bad temper, dissensions, factions" as works of the flesh (Gal. 5:19-21). In Corinth the flesh had produced two dangerous extremes concerning the proper Christian view of marriage.

Most likely the trouble started with the dyed-in-the-wool celibates. This group looked upon sex as a monstrous evil, something every spiritual Christian would shy away from. Behind their thinking undoubtedly lay the philosophical dualism of the ancient Greeks who taught that everything material was bad and everything spiritual was good. The human body, in their way of thinking, was the base and sinful part of man, while his soul was pure. A Christian should have nothing to do with the lusts of the flesh, such as sex. Their ideal was the ascetic. According to them, single people should abstain from marriage, and even Christians who are already married should take what Catholics now call a "brother-sister vow" and live in a Platonic relationship. This group would say, "Sex is dirty!"

On the other hand, the Jewish Christians in the Corinthian church, and perhaps others, reacted strongly against the point of view that sex was sin. The idea of not marrying was so uncongenial to the Jewish mentality that the Old Testament has no word for "bachelor." A godly life for them meant not only marriage, but also children. As the stories of Sarah, Anna, and Elizabeth illustrate, barrenness was considered to be a curse of God. To this group if there was any sin involved in the matter, the sin was to *refuse* to marry.

Of course the general moral atmosphere of the city of Corinth was so low that it severely hindered any calm, objective meditation on the Christian ethic of sex and marriage. As a result, all kinds of unusual ideas and practices arose. In some cases the newly-converted husband would even think he should leave his unconverted wife if she didn't receive Christ, and vice versa. Confusion reigned. Homes were being broken up while the believers argued their points of view.

There did not necessarily have to be so much trouble between those who were strong on the side of celibacy and those who were equally as strong on the side of marriage.

Each could have respected the other's point of view. But their carnality pushed the Corinthians to adopt extreme positions, meddle in each other's private lives, and fight with each other over the issues.

DOCTRINE

Facing up squarely to this difficulty, Paul sets forth four important aspects of the Christian doctrine of marriage:

1. *The purity of marriage* (7:1-9). Paul begins by pointing out that there is much room in the Christian scheme of things both for celibacy (7:1) and marriage (7:2). Both of these parties in Corinth were wrong, not because they were for or against celibacy, but because they carried their positions to carnal extremes. The celibates had a right to remain single, but they had no right to condemn others for marrying. Sex in marriage is pure from every point of view, and Paul recommends that if a person does not have a special gift for celibacy, the normal thing for him to do is to marry so that he will not have to burn inside with frustrated passions (7:9).

Outside of marriage no one has the right to use his sexual powers, but marriage gives men and women this privilege. Hebrews 13:4 says, "Let marriage be held in honor by all and the marriage bed unpolluted; for God will judge the immoral adulterous." The physical aspect of marriage isn't all privilege, however, for Paul indicates that it also carries a solemn responsibility for both parties. Wedding vows imply that both husband and wife give up exclusive rights to their own bodies, agreeing to share them fully with their partner (7:4). The happiest marriages are those characterized by complete liberty, few inhibitions, and the absence of any guilt complex. The idea that "sex is dirty" has ruined many marriages, and apparently it was doing this very thing in Corinth.

It is wrong to consider celibacy as morally superior to marriage. Unfortunately this idea has been allowed to develop in the Catholic Church and also in some Protestant thinking. For example, it underlies a great deal of the opposition to certain methods of birth control even today. It also leads to requiring a vow of chastity from priests and religious orders. Admittedly celibacy has its *practical* advantages over marriage, and these Paul brings out later, but there is certainly no *moral* advantage involved (7:5). There are both spiritual and carnal married folk, and there are both spiritual and carnal celibates.

2. *The permanence of marriage* (7:10, 11). Undoubtedly, the ideal situation is that both partners in a marriage be Christians. But while young people can and should choose Christian partners for a future marriage, this is impossible when either the husband or wife of an already existing marriage is converted. Apparently in Corinth, new converts were leaving their partners and breaking up their homes.

When it comes right down to it, there is no essential difference between a Christian marriage in a church and a pagan marriage in the living room of a justice of the peace. As a matter of fact, the terms "Christian" and "pagan" as applied to marriage itself have little more meaning than a "Christian" bottle of milk or a "pagan" bottle of milk. There are marriages between Christians and marriages which produce Christian homes, but marriage is not a sacrament over which the church has a monopoly as some think. It is a human institution decreed by God, and is to be observed by the whole human race. When two people sincerely agree to live with each other, have a home and family, and obey the social norms for marriage in their particular community, they are husband and wife in the sight of God regardless of their religion.

God's will is that everyone's marriage be permanent, no matter who is involved. While it is possible for a marriage bond to be broken by unfaithfulness (Matt. 19:9), it is certainly not what God desires. Nor does He desire that the conversion of one of the partners precipitate the breakup of a happy home. This leads us to the next point . . .

3. *The power of marriage* (7:12-16). Instead of leaving his family, a Christian should constantly strive to win his

loved ones to the Lord. When Christianity enters a non-Christian home, it should be a source of new blessing, not of new grief. The unbelieving wife or husband is in some sense "sanctified" by living in the same house as a Christian (7:14). There is no reason for the Christian to leave.

The marriage relationship is a powerful tool in the hands of God for salvation. When a man is converted, if he is the head of the house as he should be, his family usually finds the Lord soon. This was the case with the Philippian jailer and Cornelius. But often when a woman becomes a Christian, she has to be content with a slower process. Many women make the mistake of trying to argue their husbands into accepting the Lord, but this is not the best way to go about it. Peter says that wives should submit themselves to their husbands: the husbands will more readily be won to Christ this way than through their wives' preaching (I Peter 3:1, 2), which can too easily be construed as nagging. The best quality in a Christian wife is not to preach a good sermon, but to make a happy home for her husband and provide for his physical, emotional, and sexual needs.

There are times when the heart of the unbelieving partner becomes so hardened that he leaves the believer. Paul says that "the brother or the sister is under such circumstances not tied down" (7:15). Does this mean that the abandoned believer may remarry? Bible scholars are not in agreement as to the answer, but those who think they may remarry call this the "Pauline privilege." Along with adultery, it is considered as one of the sins which may end a marriage prematurely. If the marriage is truly ended, presumably the partners become single again, and the possibility of remarriage then opens up.

Children who have one or two Christian parents are at a great advantage over those reared in non-Christian homes. Paul says they are "dedicated" (7:14). He does not mean that they are automatically saved just by being born in a Christian home, but they undoubtedly will hear the Gospel at an early age and most likely commit their lives to Christ. Paul assumes that Christian parents will be faithful in providing spiritual teaching for their children. Unfortunately, many parents today lavish abundant food and expensive gifts on their children but totally fail to provide them the spiritual food necessary for their development.

4. *The privilege of chastity* (7:17-40). Marriage and a family is the normal state of affairs for Christians and non-Christians alike. But to certain members of the body of Christ, God gives the special gift of celibacy (7:7). When celibacy is seen as a spiritual gift, or charisma, parallel to the gifts of pastor, apostle, teacher, prophecy, helps, etc., many difficulties that are otherwise raised concerning it disappear. Most Christians, for example, are not pastors, but those who do have the gift consider it a privilege. By the same token, those who have the gift of remaining single should consider it an equal privilege. The parable of the talents indicates that whatever our gift or gifts may be, we should be thankful and use them to the glory of God.

Sometimes we tend to feel that there is something wrong with a Christian who is an "old maid" or a "confirmed bachelor." Paul is not in agreement. He says that an unmarried man is "concerned with the Lord's affairs," but that a married man "is concerned with things of the world, how to please his wife" (7:32, 33). This same applies to a woman (7:34). No one who has a family to care for will deny that marriage and children are time consuming, that they tie a person down, and that they do not permit full attention to be given to the Lord's work. They know they cannot do as much for God as a single person, but this is not usually a source of frustration. The Bible teaches that marriage and family responsibilities are God's will for the majority of human beings (Gen. 2:24). Those who do not have the gift of celibacy would be less effective for the Lord single than married.

The Christian man or woman who has the gift of chastity should feel honored, and should be diligent in using it. In the church, on the mission field, and in other aspects of God's work, there are many jobs which can be handled most easily and efficiently by single people. Too often social pressures create a feeling of frustration in a person who would otherwise be happy and well-adjusted as a single person. God does not want celibacy to become a source of unhappiness for anyone.

Does all this mean that the Catholic Church is right in making celibacy a requirement for priests and nuns? Protestants have never been in agreement and recently many Catholic leaders are themselves having second thoughts. The fact that Peter, supposedly the first pope, was married makes the Catholic position an uncomfortable one. So does Paul's statement, "A bishop must be . . . the husband of only one wife . . . keeping his children under control with complete respect" (I Tim. 3:2, 4). Protestants have realized all along that celibacy is a special gift, but never obligatory for full-time Christian service. It is a privilege, but not a prerequisite. In the process of *aggiornamento* it seems that the Catholic church will eventually change its position.

DECISION

Implicit in the *doctrine* of marriage which Paul expounds is found his *decision*. He draws several practical conclusions:

1. If you have the gift of celibacy do not seek to be married but rather use your gift as a single person for God's glory. "To the single and the widows, I say that it is good for them to remain as I am" (7:8).

2. If you do not have the gift of celibacy, plan to marry. If you don't marry, you'll most likely get into trouble either inwardly or outwardly. "But because of prevailing immoralities let every man have his own wife and let every woman have her own husband" (7:2). Saying this does not imply that you should marry the first person who appears interested. Leave the choice of a partner and the timing in God's hands.

3. If you are getting married, be sure your prospective husband or wife is a Christian. Marry "only in the Lord" (7:39, KJV). Unless you live in one of those increasingly rare places where no Christian partners are available, you

should go slowly about getting emotionally involved with an unbeliever. This does not mean that a casual date with an unbeliever is always wrong. Many have led their future spouses to the Lord during courtship. But if no interest in the things of God is sincerely shown, it is probably a sign that the individual is not God's choice for a life partner. Break it off before it is too late.

4. If you are already married to an unbeliever, make any sacrifice to preserve the marriage. It might be a difficult situation, but bear the cross. You might well win your husband or wife to the Lord by so doing (7:12-16).

5. If you want a happy marriage, don't neglect to provide for your partner all the physical satisfaction he or she needs. The wife owns her husband's body and the husband owns his wife's body (7:4). The Bible fully recognizes the sexual relationship as one of the most sublime expressions of marital love. The only exception to this might be termed "sexual fasting" as described in 7:5. This is temporary abstention from sex with mutual consent for the purpose of prayer. Like fasting from food, it should not be overdone either in frequency or duration.

In a day when loose moral standards seem to be threatening the existence of marriage, the home, and the family, Christians should be aware of the fact that God still has high requirements and that He expects Christians to live up to them. Doing so will result in a fruitful and well-adjusted life whether single or married. There are few better ways of understanding God's standards for sex and marriage than quiet meditation on Paul's counsel in First Corinthians 7.

Study Questions

1. Dualistic philosophy (absolute distinction between the flesh and the spirit) gave carnal license to some Corinthians, and caused an opposite reaction in others. Today a similar philosophy is at work in the United States. Can you give some examples?

2. Within the Catholic Church a strong debate is raging over whether priests and nuns should be required to take vows of celi-

bacy or not. In the light of I Corinthians 7, what is your opinion?

3. Discuss your views on the nature of divorce. How do you answer the question: can a divorced person remarry? What are your reasons?

4. What attitude does your church take toward single women? What vital part can they play in their church and society better than a married person?

6

Meat, Movies, and Miniskirts

I Corinthians 8-10

THE AVERAGE CHRISTIAN does not have much trouble in distinguishing between things that are really good and things that are really bad. But when it comes to that wide, slippery no-man's land of doubtful issues, most of us start to scratch our heads. Go to church on Sunday? That's fine! Commit adultery? That's out! These are black-and-white issues, and they don't ordinarily cause serious problems, at least in the sense in knowing right from wrong.

But how about movies? dancing? smoking? a social drink? Sunday fun? necking? cards? miniskirts? Now the picture fades from black and white to varying shades of gray. In many cases Christians even in the same church, not to mention different parts of the country, cannot agree as to whether these and other similar ethical issues are legitimate pursuits for Christians or not.

Back in Corinth there may not have been many arguments about movies or miniskirts, but they had the same type of problems. The main point of contention was — of all things — eating meat.

Although it may seem strange to us, one of the serious temptations for the first-century Corinthian believers involved worshiping an idol. No one had a question in his mind that idol worship was a sin. No spiritual Christian would do it. That was as easy as black and white.

But the shades of gray appeared when some of the cultural overflow of idol worship on the part of others spilled over and touched the Christians. How about eating some of the meat that the pagans had offered to their idols? Could that be harmful? Can a Christian do it? Was eating the meat the same as worshiping the idol to which it was sacrificed? Might it be what the Bible calls an appearance of evil?

It is true that eating sacrificial meat poses no problem for us today. But First Corinthians 8-10, which deals with this problem in detail, is extremely important because it gives us basic principles of Christian ethics which will help us decide any doubtful issue that may touch our lives. And no Christian I have ever met is free from this kind of problem.

Eating meat is what is known as an amoral issue. This must be kept in mind for a full understanding of this section. It is neither moral, like loving one's neighbor, nor immoral, like murder. In itself it has no good or bad qualities. Only the implications which people attach to it can color it with ethical significance one way or the other. If we capture the doctrinal insights that God has for us in these chapters, we will be able to resolve any amoral problem that for one reason or another may bother us. For the Corinthians it was meat. For us, it may be movies, or miniskirts, or you name it. . . .

Difficulty

What were the Corinthians up against? With the exception of the relatively small Jewish colony in the city, the whole population of Corinth practiced idolatry. It was the national religion. The worship of idols and all that went along with it (don't forget the temple of Aphrodite!), had become part of the very warp and woof of their lives, especially of their moral activities.

The occasion of a family reunion, or any other excuse

for a major party, was usually tied up with an idol feast of some kind or other. Converts to Christianity immediately renounced the religious aspects of idolatry, recognizing that the idol was no god at all, but rather an inanimate object. But the social aspects of idolatry still presented thorny problems to them. This involved three places in particular where the Corinthians might obtain idol meat and thus enmesh themselves in suspicions that they had gone back to worshiping idols.

The first place was in the idol temples themselves. The person throwing the party might buy a steer and turn it over to the priest to prepare for the feast. The priest would butcher the animal, burn the fat and the entrails as a sacrifice to the chosen idol, then use the rest of the steer as food for the cultic banquet. The priest himself might retain a portion of the meat in payment for his services. If not all the meat were used in the banquet, the surplus would be sold wholesale to the butchers in the public market. The most luxurious of the idol feasts were held right in the temples, then, and sometimes Christian friends or relatives would be invited.

The second place where the Corinthians traditionally ate idol meat was in private homes. Some, rather than assume the expense of a banquet in the temple, would bring the meat home after the sacrifice and invite their friends there. While this was out of sight of the idol itself, the meat served was identical to that served in the temple. Could a Christian accept an invitation to such a social gathering?

Finally, the public markets themselves were full of sacrificed meat. Both the worshiper and the priest would often sell surplus parts of the sacrificed animal to local butchers, and since the chosen victims had to be without blemish, this was likely to be the best meat of all. Of course it was impossible to distinguish sacrificed from unsacrificed meat on the butcher's hooks. This situation left scrupulous Christian housewives in a quandary when they went shopping.

Remember that the dominant spiritual quality of the Corinthians was, unfortunately, carnality. The same carnality that led them to divide into four parties, to be overly tolerant of sin in their midst, and to distort God's standards for sex and marriage, led them also to take rather extreme positions on the issue of idol meat. Bitter quarrels arose among them. Some had rock-firm convictions against eating any kind of idol meat, no matter where it was found. The converted Jews would understandably tend to feel this way. They would eat nothing but kosher meat. They were undoubtedly joined in their abstinence by many who before their conversion had been particularly fanatic idolaters.

As missionaries have frequently reported, religious zeal seems to be an underlying personality trait which is usually carried over from one religion to another. A fanatic pagan will usually become a fanatic Christian (or anti-pagan) when he is converted, whereas a moderate pagan will tend to become a moderate Christian as a general rule.

It is easy to see, then, that the worst of the idolaters would naturally move to the other extreme and totally reject anything they considered a vestige of pagan religion. They would rather become vegetarians for the rest of their lives than take the chance of swallowing a mouthful of idol meat! This is much like some converted Roman Catholics who cannot worship in a church no matter how evangelical otherwise, where a lighted candle is part of the decor. Their basic mistake is to ascribe *moral* values to *amoral* issues. Whenever this is done, trouble is in store.

The group that opposed them was carnal also, but their thinking was clearer. They rightly identified eating meat as an amoral issue, and therefore were able to look at the problem less passionately. They had rejected idolatry, but at the same time they did not see anything wrong with eating meat that may have been sacrificed to an idol if their hearts were right with God. After all, wasn't an idol just a piece of carved stone? What difference did it make if the steer was butchered in front of a stone or out in a field or in a slaughterhouse? The meat was the same anyway. These people went ahead and ate the meat where and when they pleased, even in the temples themselves. By doing so, they infuriated their brethren who thought that eating meat was im-moral.

Paul, in First Corinthians 8-10, labels the group of ab-stainers "weak" (8:10). He doesn't use the word "strong" in this section, but it would not be an illegitimate inference to conclude that Paul thought of the opposing group of those who indulged in the meat as "strong" Christians.

In almost every Christian Church in the world you will find weak and strong Christians. If the church is spiritual, they will be living together in harmony and fellowship. This is the way it should be. There is nothing sinful about being either weak or strong. The body of Christ is made up of both. Sin enters the picture only when the weak and the strong begin to quarrel and thereby break fellowship. This is what happens when the church is carnal like the Corinthian church. Trouble will inevitably arise, and then express it-self in the form of a two-headed monster. The weak Chris-tians will judge the strong as being worldly, and the strong Christians will hold the weak in contempt as being fanatical or pharisaical. The best expression of this is found in Ro-mans 14:3 where Paul says, "The one who eats should not feel contempt for him who abstains, nor should the one who abstains censure him who eats; for God has accepted him."

Carnality will make each group consider itself spiritually superior to the other. This is a curious but important fact. The point is that whether a Christian is weak or strong in the sense we have been mentioning is not directly related to his spirituality. It can usually be traced to his psychological, emotional and religious background, even to his own at-titudes before he was converted. Conversion does not make everyone strong or everyone weak. There are weak Chris-tians who are carnal and others who are spiritual. There are strong Christians who are carnal and others who are spir-itual.

The factor that really makes the difference between spir-ituality and carnality is never knowledge. It is love. Again, the Corinthians' basic difficulty comes down to their lack of Christian love.

DOCTRINE

As his starting point in the *doctrinal* section, (8:1—10:
24), Paul begins with a contrast between knowledge and
love. If you go through Chapter 8, you will see that these
two threads run parallel throughout the chapter. The superior knowledge of the strong Christians who weren't particularly troubled by the idol meat is mentioned in verses 1,
2, 4, 7, 10, and 11. The love that should have tempered
their knowledge is brought out in verses 1, 3, 7, 10, and 12.
Without knocking knowledge, which is a good thing to
have, Paul clearly warns that it becomes worthless when it is
not combined with Christian love. "Knowledge *puffs* up,
but love *builds* up" (8:1).

This section is addressed to the strong, rather than to the
weak group at Corinth. Perhaps they were the ones who
wrote Paul about their problem. The most significant ethical
principle that Paul brings out is the entire concept of the
weaker brother.

One of the most interesting aspects of Paul's procedure
is that he does not invoke the decision of the Jerusalem
Council, which included the stipulation, "that you abstain
from food offered to idols" (Acts 15:29). The evidence
indicates that while Paul was happy that he won his point
about not requiring circumcision of the Gentiles who became Christians, he was not altogether pleased with the
other aspects of the Council decision. He probably considered that they were an overly simple and perhaps legalistic
effort to solve a complex ethical problem. These borderline
cases are never black and white and there is no pat answer
for them. Paul declares that eating meat is an amoral problem, and that in itself it is neither good nor bad (8:8). By
doing so, he at once admits that the problem is more complex
than the Jerusalem Council would have considered it, for
they treated it as something not amoral, but immoral.
Whereas Paul might have dismissed the issue with a sentence or two quoted from Jerusalem, instead he dedicated
three whole chapters to developing the ethical principles

underlying the Christian attitude toward amoral issues.

If these strong Christians had been living by themselves on a desert island somewhere, they could eat the meat to their hearts' content and not be any worse off spiritually than if they had abstained. But this is not so simple when you live in a Christian community with others who may not be in full agreement with you. When there are weaker brethren in the same church (and there usually are), this factor must temper and guide the superior knowledge that the strong Christian has. He must not only consider his own feelings in the matter, but he must also be careful not to offend his weaker brother or place a stumbling block in his path (8: 7, 9). One danger of this is that the weaker brother might be encouraged to act against his own conscience, and therefore commit a sin (8:10-12). This would reveal an unfortunate lack of love in the heart of the strong Christian.

Paul, who identifies himself with the strong segment because he himself recognizes an amoral issue when he sees it, sums up the whole matter in his own personal rule of life: "If my eating causes my brother to stumble, I shall eat no meat forever, so that my brother will not be made to fall into sin" (8:13). As we shall see later, this does not mean that a Christian must bow to certain absurd convictions that some people have developed, but it is a valid and useful norm for Christian behavior.

In chapters 9 and 10 we find two illustrations of this principle: a positive one (Paul himself) and a negative one (Israel). Let's take a closer look.

Paul begins by claiming certain rights which he could have exercised at any moment (9:1-14). He could have eaten meat (9:4), he could have married (9:5), he could have taken a salary for his work (9:5-14). Morally there would have been nothing wrong with any of these things and Paul admits that many others properly did them. But in spite of that, Paul voluntarily abstained from all three (9:15-18), at least in Corinth. He did so because he loved his weaker brethren and did not want to offend them in the least. If caution in amoral issues is required of all Christians, it is required even moreso of Christian leaders.

Christian flexibility is the watchword. Paul was a big enough man to adjust to changing circumstances. "I have become everything to everybody," he proclaims (9:22). This means that when he was in a community where there was a strong feeling against eating meat, he let it go ("to the weak I have become weak"), but where such a feeling did not exist, he undoubtedly ate it ("to those who are without law I am as without law"). Paul applied the principle of flexibility when he circumcised Timothy (Acts 16:3), but staunchly refused to circumcise Titus (Gal. 2:1-10). Nothing in this life should be so important to a Christian that he is unwilling to give it up if the law of love so demands.

Paul's second illustration, the case of Israel, the people of God, brings out another danger inherent in the attitude of strong Christians. Not only must they beware of offending their weaker brethren, but they should also be careful that their liberal attitude toward *amoral* issues does not carry them over into the sphere of issues that are *immoral*. This is one of the root errors of those who have embraced the "new morality" in our own day. Israel, for example, had superb spiritual advantages (10:1-4), but these did not prevent her from falling into such sins as idolatry and fornication (10: 7, 8). This is given as a warning to strong Christians. If you play with fire, you are liable to get burned.

DECISION

From here Paul moves from his *doctrinal* section to the actual *decision* in regard to the Corinthians' problem. As we analyze it, keep in mind that the same type of decision that Paul makes concerning meat will also apply to problems such as movies and miniskirts, although the details will naturally vary.

Paul makes separate decisions for each one of the places where the Corinthians could eat idol meat. The first is in the temples themselves. Here Paul puts his foot down, and says in effect that eating meat right under the shadow of the idol is going too far. By participating in the feast in the presence of the idol (even though we fully understand that it is just a piece of stone) the Christian has crossed the line from an amoral practice (simply eating the meat) to a sinful practice (idolatry itself) (10:20, 21). This is a case when action which is *essentially amoral* becomes in a certain context *functionally immoral*. For that reason, it is prohibited.

On the other extreme, the meat which is bought in the butcher shops should not be a matter of concern. True, it may or may not have been sacrificed to an idol, but this is not important for the Christian. The scrupulous person who makes a moral issue of this has carried things too far. It is absurd to think of it as a sin. Paul counsels the Corinthians to go ahead and buy what is sold in the market no matter what someone else might say about it (10:25, 26). This aspect of the problem should not even be classified as doubtful, but as universally permitted. It is both *essentially* and *functionally amoral*.

Now when we come to eating meat in a friend's house we have a much more delicate and complex decision on our hands. Whether a Christian should do it or not depends upon the situation in which he finds himself. If no one makes an issue out of it at the time, go ahead and eat the meat (10: 27). But if someone, whether a believer or an unbeliever, calls it to your attention, it then puts your Christian testimony and also your possible influence on the conscience of the weaker brother on the firing line. In that case, it is better to abstain (10:28, 29).

Without accepting the "new morality" or "situation ethics" which tend to make *amoral* issues out of *essentially immoral* issues, at the same time we must admit that there are cases like this when a certain situation will make an *essentially amoral* practice a *relatively immoral* matter. This type of ethical decision, which is frequent in the life of a sensitive Christian, is the farthest from black and white that you can go. It keeps a Christian on his toes and aware of the need for a close walk with Jesus Christ day by day.

Keeping in mind the principles of love and the weaker brother, however, a Christian can depend on the Holy Spirit to guide him in each set of circumstances he faces. To place in simpler language what was stated in the above paragraph, it must be clarified that the Bible does not teach that all Christian ethics are relative. What the Bible declares as immoral is always immoral and does not depend upon the situation. But what is amoral might well depend on the situation. Therefore we need not explain away the Biblical teaching that in *some* areas of *amoral* issues Christian ethics are relative.

To apply this, take the matter of meat once again. To Paul, eating idol meat in one situation (when served by a friend without any questions being raised) was all right. In other situations (in the idol temple) it was wrong. He could take it or leave it and not sin in either case. But for some of the hard-core Jews who were convinced that any non-kosher meat was sinful to eat, even buying it in the marketplace would be to act against their own conscience and therefore to them be sin (8:7, 10, 12). It was not abnormal to have these differing attitudes in the same church. The only thing that was lacking in Corinth is that neither group properly respected the feelings of the other.

Now take something more up to date like movies. As a medium of communication, movies are amoral. With the virtual abolition of motion picture censorship, many films are being shown to the public that are unquestionably pornographic. For most Christians, such films are not amoral, but immoral. Like eating meat in the temples, they should be prohibited. On the other hand, the church for years has been making good use of this medium for the glory of God. It seems that seeing a Moody Science film or films such as *Martin Luther* would, like buying meat in the market, never be considered other than amoral or might even be considered virtuous. This is a profitable way for a Christian to spend his time.

However, when we come to the films that are neither pornographic on one hand nor specifically Christian on the other, disagreement among Christians enters the picture. Some Christians think that they should never patronize a commercial theater. Others think that they can, but that they should be selective with their movies just as they are with their literature. This is where relativity comes in, and decisions should be made on the principles of love and the weaker brother. If the general feeling of your church or denomination is that a Christian should not attend, you should conform to it. No movie is worth a church split or even a serious quarrel.

Let's use miniskirts as our final example. This is a matter of fashion and I realize that maxiskirts may be "in" by the time many read this book. At any rate, miniskirts seem to some Christians as bordering on indecent exposure. The question is in the area of fashion, and how closely a Christian may conform to fashion. To mention one extreme, bare breasts would be considered as indecent exposure by virtually every Christian in our society (although they wouldn't be so considered in certain parts of Africa, for example), so topless bathing suits or see-through blouses would be out for any Christian lady. They would rightly be considered as one fashion that is immoral. On the other hand, the insistence of some missionaries who work in tropical climates that all women wear sleeves in their dresses and nylon stockings is, like meat in the market, absurd. Bare calves and arms should not be a question of conscience in our Western culture. But the exact height of the hemline, the amount of the makeup, or the length of a man's sideburns, enter into the area of relative choice. In any style change, a good rule of thumb is that the Christian need not be among the first to change, but neither should he be among the last to change.

The list of doubtful or amoral issues in today's churches is a long one. Some items affect us more than others, depending upon where we live and what church we belong to. But the principles brought out in these chapters will serve as a guide for us whatever the situation. It is well worth the effort to master them and apply them to each case. As we do, we will more and more appreciate the fact that the Corinthian church of almost 2000 years ago was really quite a contemporary church.

Study Questions

1. Explain how Paul could teach that sometimes you could eat meat, but at other times you could not eat the same meat without being inconsistent.

2. Define what is meant by strong and weak Christians. Give examples of each from among Christians you know (without mentioning names). Is being weak or strong any reflection of their spirituality?

3. Make a list of the ethical issues among Christians in your area which seem to be doubtful — neither thoroughly right nor thoroughly wrong. Then see if you can fit each item somewhere into this outline:

    A. Like meat in the market — go ahead and do it without making a fuss.

    B. Like meat in the idol temples — never do it.

    C. Like meat offered in a friend's home:

        1. Under certain circumstances, go ahead.

        2. Under certain other circumstances, leave it alone.

4. Be sure you can articulate the difference between this type of ethical decision on *amoral matters,* and the modern philosophy of "situation ethics."

7

Women and Wine

I Corinthians 11

WHEN YOU THINK OF IT, only the Holy Spirit could have accomplished the task of molding such divergent elements as Jews and Gentiles, patricians and slaves, Romans and barbarians, all into one body, the Church of Jesus Christ.

If this was a difficult achievement in the first-century world as a whole, it was even more so in Corinth because of the carnality in the lives of the believers. Sooner or later this carnality had to affect the church services themselves. Actually, three major problems arose in Corinth in regard to the worship services. The first concerned the place of women in the church, the second the correct meaning of the Lord's Supper, and the third the proper use of spiritual gifts.

In First Corinthians 11 Paul deals with the first two. He dedicates a much longer portion (chapters 12-14) to the thorny matter of spiritual gifts. To understand clearly what Paul is getting at in this chapter, it will be best to use our standard outline of "difficulty, doctrine, and decision" twice, once for what we have termed "women" and once for "wine."

FIRST DIFFICULTY: WOMEN

The trouble with the women (11:2-16) began with a legitimate feeling, but an illegitimate expression of it. Most of the Greek mystery religions were strictly stag. They excluded women from membership. As a matter of fact, they simply reflected the general cultural feeling in Greece that women were inferior to men — not quite as low as animals perhaps, but not on a par with men either.

Consequently, it was quite a good piece of news to women when Paul announced that Christ had died for them and that God desired their salvation just as much as that of their husbands and brothers. Christianity, unlike other religions, was not just for men. When they repented of their sins, and trusted Christ as their Savior, the women discovered by experience that spiritual regeneration operated fully in them in spite of their being the "weaker sex." This was the *legitimate* feeling.

The new taste of spiritual freedom was sweet to the Corinthian women. But they were carnal. They allowed this freedom to carry them to unfortunate extremes. This was the *illegitimate* expression. Before they knew it, it had produced a bitter reaction against them on the part of the men.

If the Corinthian women had been able to distinguish between their spiritual or religious freedom and their social status, they might not have fallen into their error. But they wrongly deduced that if God loved them just as much as He loved the men, and if He had saved them without discrimination, this automatically conferred upon them social equality. So they decided they had been downtrodden long enough, and they began a miniature social revolution among themselves. They were now ready to show the men who was boss!

The symbol of submission to men in those days was the veil with which women covered their heads and part of their faces. Any cultured woman in Corinth (as in some Eastern countries even today) would veil herself before appearing in public. The veil had become such a commonly accepted article of clothing that it not only symbolized their social position, but it also was directly associated with feminine dignity and modesty. To be seen without a veil immediately marked a woman as immoral, or at best immodest.

In spite of this, the Christian women in Corinth (at least

a significant portion of them) started a woman's liberation movement. They cried, "Off with the veil!" They ventured out on the streets uncovered and even attended the church services with bare heads. A similar type of impression would be created in your church if your pastor's wife showed up at the 11 o'clock worship service next Sunday in Bermuda shorts!

That's why Paul said, "Any woman who has her head uncovered while praying or prophesying dishonors her head" (11:5). It really amounted to a public scandal. The Christian women appeared more worldly than many of the non-Christians!

First Doctrine

Recognizing the fact that discarding the veil was only a surface indication of a more deeply-rooted problem, Paul puts his finger on the real trouble. "I want you to understand that Christ is the head of every man, that the man is the woman's head, and that God is the head of Christ" (11: 3). Submission of women to men is not something optional. It is a doctrinal principle for all societies. Although, as anthropologists tell us, different societies set up different mechanisms for the observance of this divine order of the sexes,* the basic relationship under God should not be altered. When it is, trouble is usually just around the corner.

Spiritually man and woman are on the same plane (11: 11, 12). The ancient Greeks were wrong when they assigned a second-class rating to female souls. But spiritual equality in Christ should not be carried over to justify a reversal of the social hierarchy that God has ordained for the human race He created.

God's feminine mystique places a wife under the authority of her husband. "Submission" is the key family command for the wife in the Bible (e.g., Eph. 5:24). Many marital difficulties begin when the woman attempts to "wear the

---

*Matriarchal societies may be a curious exception to this rule, but worldwide they are rare and relatively insignificant.

pants" in the family. Paul writes to Timothy, "So I would have younger widows marry again, bear children, manage their home, and afford the opponent no opportunity whatever for reviling" (I Tim. 5:14). Excelling as a wife and mother is the highest feminine achievement possible.

What is true of the family is true also of society in general. Incidents where women have assumed the masculine place of authority with any measure of success are extremely rare in the history of civilization. God may have had His Deborah and France her Joan of Arc, but these are outstanding chiefly because they are exceptions to the rule. The happiest families and smoothest-running societies are usually those which honor God's command that the man should be the head of the woman. At the time of the creation, God made Eve to be Adam's helpmeet, not vice versa.

The Corinthians discovered also that a church cannot run smoothly if the women do not take a submissive position. A church run by women is a novel and untypical spectacle. By saying this I do not wish to depreciate the women in our churches today who often pick up where the men fail. More than one church, for example, has a *women's* missionary society, but no *men's* missionary society. Unfortunately this has created the impression in some circles that missions are basically a woman's concern. In such cases, the men, not the women, are to blame for the women having to assume leadership. In Corinth, however, this was not the case. The women there were not as much concerned with getting the Lord's work done as with the heady possibility of changing their social status, and becoming "liberated."

First Decision

Paul's final decision is simply that the women should put their veils back on. Furthermore, they should continue to submit themselves to the men because the man "is the image and glory of God, but the woman is the man's glory . . . neither was man created for the woman's sake, but woman for the man's sake" (11:7, 9). No aspect of a woman's dress should ever be the cause of scandal as it was in Corinth.

Catholic women today continue the practice of wearing a veil or hat in church, while many Protestant women do not. Why is this? Protestant women say that it largely depends on where you live and what church you go to. Whereas a woman might wear a hat to church in Boston, she probably would not wear one in Los Angeles. Catholics argue that their custom conforms to a correct interpretation of the passage we are studying. Protestants, in an unusual turnabout, claim that taking Paul's decision literally today is too superficial.

The Protestants are right. As we have seen, the basic problem in Corinth wasn't wearing veils as such, but maintaining the divine order of the sexes. This is a classic case of Paul's *doctrine* (women being submissive to men) remaining constant, whereas his *decision* (wearing veils to church) is culturally-conditioned.

SECOND DIFFICULTY: WINE

As if the scandal of female immodesty in church were not enough to spoil a worshipful atmosphere, the carnality in the hearts of the Corinthian Christians even corrupted the communion services. In fact, the trouble in Corinth over the Lord's Supper ruined a lovely practice of the early church which otherwise we might still be enjoying today. This was the *agape,* the Christian love feast.

Today the love feast has so nearly passed into oblivion that few Christians even know that there is a direct reference to it in the Bible. Jude 12 says, "these are stains in your love feasts" (*agapai*). Because of the abuse of some of the early churches, hardly any church today celebrates the *agape.* A weak vestige of it does remain in many churches, however, in the traditional collection for the poor taken during the communion service.

What was the *agape?* Paul doesn't bother explaining it to the Corinthians because they knew very well what he was talking about. He simply assumes its existence in the entire passage (11:17-34).

Whenever the time came to celebrate the Lord's Supper (it was a weekly event), a complete meal would be served along with it. This was a closer reproduction of Christ's Last Supper when the symbolic elements were served along with the meal. "He took the cup after supper . . ." (11:25 NEB).

Not only did the love feast follow the Savior's example, but it also offered the well-to-do Christians a regular weekly opportunity to share some of their material goods with the poor. Undoubtedly all would bring something to the *agape,* but the rich were expected to bear the major responsibility. In that way the poorer families could enjoy at least one rather luxurious meal a week. After the supper, all would partake of the bread and wine of the Eucharist.

In the Corinthian church, however, this *agape* had degenerated as had many other aspects of public worship. Paul begins his treatment of the problem with one of the angriest outbursts of the whole epistle: "In giving these instructions, however, I do not commend you . . ." (11:17). What started out as a love feast had turned out to be a carnal orgy of squabblings, hurt feelings, and even drunkenness (11:21). There was no longer a thought of sharing with others for "everyone tries to grab his food before anyone else" (11:21 Phillips). The rich would appear with their rich meats and vintage wines and gather in one corner as a clique. They probably would also bring a pot of watery soup or some other token for the poor, but they would not share their best with them. There was no love expressed in this attitude. In one corner the well-to-do would indulge themselves in gluttony and drinking, while in another a subdued group of the poorer brethren would scramble for the leftovers.

This, of course, destroyed all possibility of properly commemorating the Lord's sacrifice in a Communion service after the meal. How the communion might have been handled after such an exhibition of worldliness is left to our imagination, but Paul says with great irritation, "What shall

I tell you? Shall I commend you? In this matter I do not commend you" (11:22).

SECOND DOCTRINE

Still, all things seem to work together for good. As a result of the misbehavior of the Corinthians we now have what many Bible students consider the most sublime treatment of the Lord's Supper in the Bible. Probably First Corinthians 11:23-29 is quoted more often in Communion liturgy than all other related passages combined. This is Paul's doctrinal section, taking us directly to the suffering and death of the Lord Jesus as the underlying principle of any Communion service. The *agape* was to be a time of fellowship, worship, and spiritual meditation, not an occasion for satisfying the desires of the flesh. The wine was to be taken to commemorate Christ's shed blood in obedience to His command. When used to such an extent that it produced drunken worshipers, the whole ceremony became a mockery.

To put it in a different way, the Corinthians had made the mistake that many of us tend to make today. Their Communion service had become man-centered rather than Christ-centered. While not many of us would go to the extremes of the Corinthians in this particular matter, we do often become very concerned about what we "get out of" the service, rather than how Christ is glorified through it. As we center our thoughts on Christ in the Communion service, we are more likely to fulfill His commandment to "love our neighbor as ourselves." The word for love in this commandment of Jesus is *agape*.

SECOND DECISION

Paul's practical decision in this case was to advise the Corinthians to "wait for one another. If anyone is hungry, let him eat at home" (11:33, 34). At the Lord's Table, each person should examine his own heart (11:28) to discover his true motives and feelings. Whether or not the *agape* is celebrated in your church, love should control the feelings and actions of each member. Paul's warning to the disobedient is rather chilling: "Whoever, therefore, eats the bread, or drinks the cup of the Lord in an unworthy manner, is a violator of the Lord's body and blood" (11:27). Who killed Jesus Christ? *You* did if you mock Him by partaking of the sacred elements with sin in your heart.

It should be noted that Paul does not abolish the *agape* as a solution to the problem. That would be throwing out the baby with the bath water. Nevertheless, somehow the church through the centuries has done just this. Where is the *agape* today? It is a lost treasure of the primitive church. Perhaps those who are dedicating much .effort to renovating the church and renewing the structures would do well to consider the restoration of this ancient practice.

As in the case of the idol meat, Paul refused to resort to the simplistic method of decreeing total abstinence as a preventative of future abuses. This has been one of the unfortunate tendencies of the Christian Church through the ages. The seventeenth-century Puritans did away with Christmas because some were making it a rowdy celebration. Some have substituted grape juice for the wine of the Lord's Last Supper. Some groups, such as the Salvation Army, have practically eliminated the celebration of Communion altogether because of possible abuses. "Temperance" is a fruit of the Spirit (Gal. 5:23), but in the original this means self-control and not total abstinence as some have imagined. Paul wanted the Corinthians to go on with the celebration of the *agape,* but with the self-control that behooves spiritual Christians, not with carnal indulgence of the lower appetites.

Women and wine. The social rebellion of the women and the disillusion at the Lord's Table had plunged the Corinthian worship services into disgrace. The third manifestation of their carnality in the public services was the misuse of spiritual gifts. Our discussion of this vital point will require the following two chapters.

Study Questions

1. Compare the modern day "women's liberation" movements to the attitudes of some Christian women in the first century who wanted to do away with the veil. Does this really amount to the same thing?

2. On the basis of Paul's doctrine in this chapter, what decision would you give concerning women's liberation today?

3. Are we today in danger of allowing our worship services to become man-centered rather than Christ-centered? Name some ways this could happen.

4. Why did Paul not simply prohibit the *agape* since it was so abused by the Corinthians? Carrying this principle to a slightly different area, would you be in favor of prohibition, for example, as a possible solution to the problem of drunken driving?

8

Spiritual Gifts: Their Use and Abuse

I Corinthians 12

IMMODESTLY DRESSED WOMEN in their meetings and drunkenness at Holy Communion were the two problems related to public worship that we examined in the last chapter. The third matter involved the use and abuse of spiritual gifts, a problem which many of us are facing even today with the growing "charismatic movement," popular in many churches of different denominations.

The Greek word "charisma" appears nine times in chapters 12-14. It means "spiritual gift." This is the key passage in the Word of God on the subject, so it is well for us to be fully informed as to what Paul teaches. Unfortunately the "charismatic movement" is commonly associated with just one of the spiritual gifts, that of speaking in tongues. There are several other gifts, however, about which Christians should be equally concerned. Sad to say, in many of our churches today not much attention is paid to the matter at all.

DIFFICULTY

Before going into the passage itself, it would be well to raise the question: are spiritual gifts for today? Some Bible teachers (perhaps in reaction against excesses in Pentecostalism or the charismatic movement) have argued that all, or at least some, of the New Testament spiritual gifts were given to the church only for use during the Apostolic Age, and that they were not intended to continue after this. The footnote in a well-known study Bible, for example, says, "Tongues and the sign gifts are to cease. . . ."

It is not my purpose to argue the point extensively here, but in all fairness I should state that I have not been able to find adequate Biblical or historical evidence which would warrant such a conclusion. I don't deny that the Bible contains some culture-bound truth (such as the matter of women wearing veils as we saw in the last chapter), but spiritual gifts in the church do not fall into that category. As a matter of fact, if a church does not possess and use spiritual gifts, it is sure to wither and die.

The real trouble is not so much whether gifts exist today (there was certainly no doubt in the Corinthians' minds), but what is our attitude toward them. The Corinthians were fortunate to have received all the spiritual gifts available (1:7), and as a result they should have had an ideal church.

Their church fell far short of being ideal, however, because of their carnal attitude toward the gifts. Carnality again was at the root of their difficulty. They allowed certain gifts to become spiritual status symbols, and from that point on their church went downhill. Paul begins this portion by saying, "Now concerning spiritual gifts, brethren, I would not have you ignorant" (KJV). Unfortunately there is widespread ignorance on the subject in our churches today, just as there was in Corinth.

DOCTRINE

Paul develops his doctrinal portion around the figure of the church as the body of Christ. This was a happy choice of metaphor, since the basic function of the human body is something just as familiar to each one of us today as it was in the first century. You don't have to study college anatomy to know that eyes see, legs walk, and teeth chew. In chapter

12 Paul takes a look at the body of Christ from three points of view: (1) its unity, (2) its diversity, and (3) its operation. We should look at these one by one.

(1) The unity of the body of Christ (12:12, 13). Paul's proposition in the section can be synthesized as follows: *there is only one body and the body is one.*

No one has two bodies. Even Siamese twins are two distinct personalities. The body of Christ also is one. "For just as the body is one . . . by one Spirit we have all been baptized into one body" (12:12, 13). With the multiplicity of denominations in Christendom today, it might be hard to prove to the skeptic that there is a basic unity in the church: nevertheless it exists.

Two factors parallel to our own bodies provide and maintain the unity of the body of Christ. The first is the blood. Superficially the unity between my foot, my earlobe, and my kidneys might be quite obscure. But the same blood nourishes these as well as all my other members. If the life-giving blood is cut off from any member, it soon perishes.

In a spiritual sense the blood of Christ is the unifying element in His body. No one enters the church without first having appropriated the atonement, the shedding of blood on the cross, in a personal way by faith. When a person does this, God makes him a new creature in Christ. The fact that each member of the body of Christ has experienced the new birth through the blood of Christ produces a strong spiritual unity.

Closely related to this is the second factor which maintains unity in the body, the spirit. The human spirit or soul cannot be localized in any one organ or limb. To a degree it is present in all members.

As to the church, the Bible says, "By one Spirit we have all been baptized into one body." While members of the body of Christ may be filled with the Holy Spirit to different degrees, no single member totally lacks the presence of the Spirit. Paul says, "Any one who does not have the Spirit of Christ, he does not belong to Him" (Rom. 8:9). This means he is not a member of the body.

Many people have joined churches and denominations, and have been baptized in water without having first been baptized by the Spirit. For this reason the true body of Christ does not always coincide with today's church membership rolls. In many evangelistic campaigns the bulk of conversions takes place in people who are already members of some local church.

If such powerful factors as the blood of Christ and the Holy Spirit work together to unify the church, why isn't this manifested today in a more tangible way? The presence of so many unconverted people in our churches is one reason. More important, however, is the presence of original sin in all Christians. If we could rid ourselves completely of the consequences of original sin, the door for organic unity would be open. But since sinless perfection is unattainable in practice, so also is the organic, visible unity of the body of Christ. For this reason complete organic ecclesiastical union is an illusion. Churchmen who are promoting such union often tend to dilute the doctrine of original sin and end up with an overly optimistic view of man.

(2) The diversity within Christ's body (12:14-26). Paul's proposition here can be summed up as: *there are many different members in the body, and all are necessary.*

Biologists have long understood the details of cell *division,* or how one cell multiplies itself to two either by mitosis or by miosis. But they know far less about cell *differentiation,* or how it is possible that from one parent cell such diverse tissues as lungs, hair, and eyeballs can eventually develop. The scientist who discovers this (if it is discoverable) will be assured of a Nobel prize.

A parallel phenomenon exists in the body of Christ. Cell division is like evangelism and church growth, while cell differentiation is like the distribution of spiritual gifts. God has chosen to use human instruments for multiplying the body of Christ by winning souls. This is visible and understandable. But He doesn't entrust the responsibility of differentiating the members one from another, by distributing spiritual gifts to any man, no matter how spiritual a Christian he might be. Paul says, "God has placed the members in the body, each particular one of them just as He saw fit" (12: 18). It is a great mystery to us why some Christians have certain gifts and others do not. Perhaps we can't understand it, but we can accept by faith that God has good reasons for the way He distributes the gifts.

When some hear for the first time that they no more control the spiritual gifts they have than they do the color of their eyes, they become confused when they read 12:31 which says "earnestly desire the more valuable spiritual gifts." This sounds like the Christian does have something to do with the gifts he receives. But part of the trouble lies in the fact that in English the form of the singular and plural commands is the same. "Earnestly desire" in Greek is plural. Here it is used in a collective sense. The difficulty, as we will recall, was that the church was having problems in the worship services. Paul's command to earnestly desire the best gifts is not, therefore, given to individual Christians, but to the church as a whole. Each church should be concerned that God gives to individuals within it the best gifts, and then allows these gifts to be used.

The body of Christ is so large and complex that its makeup is far above all human planning. God knows that the body must contain highly diversified members or else it would be a freak. "The body consists not of one but of many members" (12:14). Eyes are beautiful members, but how would we function, for example, if we were just one, 150-pound, blue eye? "If the entire body were an eye, where would the hearing come in?" (12:17).

To illustrate: my eye does a wonderful job in spotting a lovely apple, but if the apple is to fulfill its purpose in nourishing me, my eye is not enough. My hand grasps it, my mouth encloses a piece, my teeth chew it, my tongue moves it around properly, my throat swallows it, my stomach digests it, my liver contributes bile — the list could be extended almost *ad infinitum.*

No member of the body can get along without the other members. My right hand is now working perfectly well. If

I were to cut it off and place it on a chair on the other side of the room, however, it might still be my hand over there, but it would be useless because it was disjointed from the other members of the body.

Moreover, within the body teamwork is absolutely essential. "The eye cannot say to the hand, 'I do not need you' " (12:21). This leaves out any exclusivism in the church. No one person or no one group has all the truth or all the gifts.

But what happens when there is disagreement? Paul says that there should be no "discord in the body" (12:25). When points of disagreement come up, each member should consider the well-being of the other.

In my own body, for example, there is a disagreement. My palate loves radishes, but my stomach does not. The solution? I've given up radishes! Again, if I have an infection in my lung, my arm (which is not at all infected) is glad to bear the pain of the injection of antibiotics in order to protect another member of the body.

We should carry this attitude over into our churches. The fact that the Corinthians did not do this caused them serious problems. If we are not careful about looking out for the interests of other Christians, we will likewise have problems.

Decision

(3) The operation of Christ's body (12:27-31). Here Paul's proposition is as follows: *The church functions properly only when each member is exercising his gift or gifts.*

The advantage of possessing all of the gifts did not guarantee that the Corinthians would use them properly. Neither did a theoretical understanding of the doctrine of gifts. Here are some practical suggestions not only for the Corinthians, but for us as well.

Have you discovered your gift? If you are a mature Christian, you should have. Every member of the body of Christ has at least one gift, and many have more than one. God would not leave you in the dark about spiritual gifts (12:1).

You have a gift, and it is a shame if you are not using it. Some day, as the parable of the talents shows, God will hold you responsible for the gifts He has given you. He will not judge for more than you have, but whether it is one, two, or five talents, you are expected to gain a proportionate return during this life on earth. If you do, God will say "Well done, good and faithful servant."

If you have not discovered your gift, or if you are not using it, here are some concrete steps you can take toward correcting the situation:

A. Distinguish between spiritual gifts and natural talents when possible. Every human being has some natural talent or other. This should not be confused with spiritual gifts. Christians have spiritual gifts, but pagans do not. When a person is born again and becomes a member of the body of Christ, God gives him a spiritual gift or gifts for which he will be responsible. In doing this, God may use a natural talent as raw material. If a person is an excellent teacher before his conversion, for example, it is highly possible that God will give him the gift of teaching, but we should not fall into the error of considering all spiritual gifts as just souped-up talents. The gift of prophecy may be a good example of a spiritual gift which would have no natural talent as a predecessor.

B. Know the possibilities of spiritual gifts. The Bible has several lists, none of which are exhaustive. This leaves open the possibility that there are spiritual gifts that are not even mentioned in the Bible. Read I Corinthians 12, Romans 12, and Ephesians 4 in a prayerful attitude, asking God to make you understand the meaning of these gifts. Sometimes slightly different names are used for the same gift, and sometimes it is difficult to know just exactly what these gifts mean for us today. I would not want to be dogmatic at this point, but I will venture to make a basic list of nineteen gifts which are named in the Bible along with capsule definitions. We should be on the lookout for them in our churches today.

1. Apostles (missionaries, cross-cultural use of other gifts).
2. Prophets (receive direct communication from God).
3. Teachers (communicating, including preaching and writing)
4. Evangelists (unusual power in soul winning and establishing churches).
5. Pastors (care of souls in the church, including elders and bishops).
6. Ministry (helping others, *diakonía*).
7. Administration (charismatic leadership).
8. Wisdom (extraordinary judgment and perception).
9. Knowledge (information).
10. Faith (discernment of God's specific will and action upon it).
11. Exhortation (spiritual counseling that is effective).
12. Miracles (use of supernatural power).
13. Healing (apart from known medical practices).
14. Tongues (ecstatic utterance).
15. Interpretation (understanding the message in tongues).
16. Discerning of spirits (recognition of authentic gifts in some and phoniness in others).
17. Giving (liberality over and above what is normally required).
18. Mercy (compassion for others).
19. Continence (see chapter 5).

C. Trust God to give you all the gifts you should have, and then to show you not only what your gifts are, but also what they are *not*. Equal to the tragedy of a Christian who does not know what gifts he has is the Christian who is frustrated because he is trying to use a gift that he has never received. God might show you, for example, that you do not have the gift of evangelist. This naturally does not excuse you from being a good witness wherever you go, and to be alert to win souls when the opportunity presents itself. This common denominator is expected of every Christian. But some members of the body of Christ find themselves particularly successful in personal evangelism and others in public evangelism. It is a fallacy to think that every Christian, if he just applied himself enough, or prayed enough, or was filled with the Holy Spirit enough, or read his Bible enough, could be another Billy Graham. Remember the 150-pound eye? Many people who are outstanding evangelists are in turn failures as pastors, simply because they do not have the necessary gift for that type of ministry.

D. Be content with what you have, and be content with what other brethren have. All gifts are necessary to get the job done properly. I can't operate my typewriter with my feet, but neither can I walk up to it on my hands. We must be careful to avoid expecting others to have our gifts. A writer who says that anyone can do it if he tries hard enough is fooling himself and frustrating his brother. Some professors of personal evangelism in Bible schools obviously have the gift of evangelism themselves, but they become irritated with their students who do not have the same gift and who therefore cannot match their professor in effective soul winning.

We must also avoid envying others because they have gifts that we don't have. This can cause such an inferiority complex that a person begins to attempt to give himself a gift instead of waiting for the Holy Spirit to do it. This form of carnality, often subconscious, shows up, for example, in many missionary dropouts. Somehow they are deceived into thinking they have the gift of the missionary, but after arriving on the field they find to their dismay that they do not have it.

Finally, one of the most subtle temptations related to spiritual gifts is a two-sided coin. The first side is to take self-pride in the gifts that God has given you as if they imply some merit on your part. The other side is to be so "humble" that you refuse to admit you have any gifts at all, and thereby never get around to using them. Both attitudes are wrong, and will have to be accounted for at the judgment seat of Christ.

E. Once you know what your gift is, develop it. "Keep alive the flame of God's gracious gift that is in you," Paul writes to Timothy (II Tim. 1:6). This is where diligent study and practice come in. If you have the gift of teaching, take specialized studies in pedagogy. If you have the gift of liberality (the gift of giving), study finances in order to make the Lord's money stretch as far as possible. Good preparation is not unspiritual and will stand any Christian in good stead for a lifetime of using his spiritual gifts fruitfully.

Some of us have gone through the painful experience of having children born with brain damage. Since they do not function as they should, parents are understandably grieved. But I have often wondered if God isn't grieved in a similar way when He sees His children not functioning as they should as members of His church. If we were all to promise God that we would make a sincere effort to discover and utilize our gifts to the full, the Christian Church would undergo a revolution.

But this does not conclude the matter. The Corinthians were using gifts as spiritual status symbols, and the chief culprit was the gift of tongues. This is important enough to warrant a separate chapter.

Study Questions

1. How can carnality nullify the effectiveness of spiritual gifts?
2. Obviously, the gifts which God has given to the members of the body of Christ are not being used to any large extent in our churches today. Can you suggest some reasons why this is true?
3. Which of the gifts on p. 94 has God given you? Have you been using them? What are you doing to develop them toward more effectiveness in the future?
4. How can the doctrine of spiritual gifts (1) avoid false humility? (2) reduce spiritual pride? (3) eliminate envy?

9

Charismatics in Corinth

I Corinthians 13, 14

WAS THE CORINTHIAN CHURCH a Pentecostal church?

This is an interesting question in spite of the fact that it is impossible to use twentieth-century denominational labels for first-century churches. But regardless of what the Corinthian church's denominational affiliation might have been today, one thing is certain: the gift of tongues (a widespread phenomenon there) and *glossolalia* (Greek for tongues-speaking) were common in their church services as they are in many Pentecostal churches today.

DIFFICULTY

Speaking in tongues figures in almost all the Biblical lists of spiritual gifts. It should have been received by the Christians and used for the building up of the body of Christ along with all the others. But instead of edifying the church, tongues caused nothing but trouble among the Corinthians. Somehow they had the idea that speaking in tongues was the best of all spiritual gifts. Those who spoke in tongues were considered to be the first-class Christians, and those who did not were considered rather second rate. The difficulty did not spring from the possession of the gift of tongues but rather in how it was being used.

97

First Corinthians 13 is well known as the most exalted passage on love in the Bible. But surprisingly few Christians have come to understand this chapter in its original context. What does this great love chapter have to do with the trouble the Corinthians were having with their spiritual gifts?

The key is found in 12:31, "Earnestly desire the more valuable spiritual gifts. And I shall show you a still more excellent way." The more excellent way is love. Some have fallen into the careless error of speaking of "the gift of love." Love is not a spiritual gift at all. It is on a plane far above all the spiritual gifts. Love is the *fruit* of the Spirit (Gal. 5:22). If we clearly see the difference between the gifts and the fruit of the Spirit, we will at once understand why the Corinthians were in such trouble.

As we saw in the previous chapter, spiritual gifts are distributed among members of the body of Christ according to the designs and purposes of God Himself. As a result each Christian will have one or more of the gifts, but probably never all of them. On the other hand, the fruit of the Spirit should be fully manifested in the life of *every* Christian without exception. It is quite possible that I could have the gift of teaching, for example, but not the gifts of pastor or evangelist. But if I am a mature Christian, no matter what my spiritual gifts may be, I should constantly manifest love, joy, peace, longsuffering, and all that is involved in the fruit of the Spirit.

In other words, there is a direct relationship between one's sanctification and the *fruit* of the Spirit in his life, but there is no such relationship between sanctification and the possession of spiritual *gifts*. The proof of this is evident in the case of the Corinthians. They had all the spiritual gifts available (1:7), but still they ended up as the most carnal church described in the New Testament (3:1).

Sanctification (which is the theological term for a close walk with Jesus Christ) will make all the difference in the world as to how effectively a Christian *uses* his gift, but it never determines which gifts he might have. Here was the Corinthians' main error. They gauged a person's spiritual life by whether he spoke in tongues, not by the love he expressed in his practical life. This provoked Paul to write his immortal chapter on love which begins, "Even though I speak in human and angelic language and have no love, I am as noisy brass or a clashing cymbal." He is saying that whereas spiritual gifts are good and necessary for the church (chapter 12), without love to govern them they become worthless.

Since the Corinthians' most serious error in the realm of spiritual gifts involved their attitude toward tongues, Paul found it necessary to write First Corinthians 14 on the subject. Here we find a solid doctrinal section which should guide our thinking at all times.

DOCTRINE

The first question that comes up is: Just what was the nature of the tongues in the Corinthian church? Were they understandable human languages, or were they ecstatic utterances which have no relationship to human languages? This point has been widely debated in recent years by those who have studied the neo-pentecostal movement, and arguments have been given on both sides.

My own conclusion is that the tongues in First Corinthians 14 were unintelligible ecstatic utterances, in contrast to the tongues on the day of Pentecost recorded in Acts 2 where they are described as real human languages. The reasons are as follows:

1. Tongues in the Book of Acts was part of the unique historical event which, when concluded, was not to be repeated. The fulfillment of Christ's promise of the coming of the Holy Spirit (John 16:7-15) occurred as a *sequence of events,* not on one day only.

Many people think of the day of Pentecost and nothing more as the fulfillment of this promise. This is too limited a view. It seems to me that the second filling with the Holy Spirit in Jerusalem (Acts 4:31), the conversion of the Samaritans (Acts 8:14-18), the conversion of the first Gentiles in Cornelius' house (Acts 10:44-48), and the enlightenment of the disciples of John the Baptist (Acts 19:1-7) are not events isolated from Pentecost. They should be taken together with Acts 2 to form what could be called "the Pentecostal Event." Once the Pentecostal Event with all its subphases was completed, it was never to occur again. Christ's promise had been fulfilled. The Holy Spirit had come to the church once for all.

In three of the cases cited above, the Bible mentions that tongues were spoken (Pentecost, Cornelius' house, and Ephesus), but there is no reason to think they weren't involved in the other two events also. The point is that in one of the five events (Pentecost) we are clearly told what kind of tongues they were — true human languages. "How is it, then, that we each hear them in our native speech in which we were born?" (Acts 2:8). By inference the same was probably true of the other phases of the Pentecostal event.

2. The tongues in Corinth, however, were not the same kind. The Pentecostal Event had passed into history and the Corinthian church was participating in a new, post-Pentecostal development of the church. Nowhere does Paul mention that tongues in Corinth would have been understandable to foreigners who happened to be in the same meeting. They were no longer signs of the *coming* of the Holy Spirit, but rather they now figured in a list of nineteen *gifts* of the Holy Spirit which God was distributing throughout the Body of Christ, presumably for the duration of the whole church age.

A similar distinction applies to the baptism in the Holy Spirit. The spiritual baptism received by those who participated in the Pentecostal event was unique and does not need to be repeated in our lives today. Our spiritual baptism is described in First Corinthians 12:13, "For by one Spirit we have all been baptized into one body."

Paul's contrast of tongues to prophecy shows even more clearly that the tongues in First Corinthians were ecstatic utterances. He makes the point that in public meetings prophecy is a more valuable gift than tongues (14:1) because "he who prophesies gives people a constructive, encouraging and comforting message" (14:3). Prophecy made sense to all hearers, tongues did not. As a matter of fact the person who spoke in tongues didn't even know what he was saying himself. "For whoever speaks in a tongue does not speak to men but to God; no one catches the meaning; he is uttering secret matters in the Spirit" (14:2). "In case I pray in a tongue, my spirit prays, but *my mind is unproductive*" (14:14).

3. At the risk of stretching a point a little, it seems to me that a careful reading of First Corinthians 13:1 will confirm that the division between these two classes of tongues is real. "Even though I speak in human (Pentecostal Event) and angelic language (Corinthian tongues). . . ." Tongues as a spiritual gift could not be understood any place on earth. Could it be that they are the language that angels speak, supernaturally given to some Christians?

4. Linguists have made tape recordings of tongues as spoken by those in the charismatic movement today and have submitted them to linguistic analysis. They report that no structure typical of a human language can be discerned. Nevertheless, some reliable witnesses report cases in which a person *has* spoken in a human language which he has not known before, and which was perfectly understood by someone present as on the day of Pentecost. There is no reason to deny that this may have happened and that it may happen again. If it does, however, it would probably be better to attribute it to a special miracle worked by the Holy Spirit on a particular occasion or in a particular life, rather than to consider it a normal expression of the gift of tongues.

If tongues, then, were an ecstatic utterance, we can more readily understand why Paul tells the Corinthians to use them privately. There would have been no problem in the church if they had confined speaking to God to their quiet times. The problem was caused by speaking in tongues in the public meetings. No one understood what the speaker was saying, with the possible exception of a person who had the complementary gift of interpretation. It should be noted that this gift of interpretation does not refer, say, to an Oriental who was traveling through Greece and who understood his own native language. It involved a supernatural understanding of "angelic language." The gift of interpretation (not to be confused with translation) was essential if the message in tongues was to result in the edification of the congregation as a whole.

DECISION

What good are tongues, then? In his decision, Paul comes to three conclusions:

In the first place, tongues are a good gift and they should not be prohibited. "Do not hinder the speaking with tongues" (14:39). Paul said, "Thanks be to God, I speak in tongues more than all of you" (14:18). Just because of possible abuses of the gift, it shouldn't be thrown out altogether. As in the case of the *agape,* total abstinence is seldom the best solution to the problem of excess. Nevertheless, tongues is not the best gift for edifying the church — prophecy, for example, is much better. "In the congregation I would rather speak five words intelligibly (prophecy) to instruct others than a myriad of words in a tongue" (14:19).

In the second place, tongues should be used in public only when an interpreter is present. This evidently caused much trouble in Corinth, and it is one of the major faults of the tongues movement today. Those who lead public meetings should be strict in not permitting a message in tongues if it is not to be interpreted for the edification of the whole group. "But in case there is no interpreter, let them keep still in the church" (14:28).

In the third place, tongues are good for a personal spiritual experience with the Lord privately. Paul says, "He who speaks in a tongue improves himself" (14:4). If there is no interpreter in the church, let him "speak to himself and to God" (14:28). The personal testimony of many who have the gift of tongues is that through it they have enjoyed a fellowship with God more intimate than they had ever known before.

Now this brings us to a point which plagues many Christians today, especially those who have friends in the charismatic movement. Are those who have not spoken in tongues second-rate Christians? In Corinth this feeling was prevalent, and unfortunately it continues to cause problems in many churches today. The answer is a most emphatic "no!" Tongues is not a *fruit* of the Spirit (like love) which everyone is to have. It is a *gift* of the Spirit which only selected members of the body have. Those who do not *love* are second-rate Christians because love is a fruit of the Spirit. It is absurd to attempt to apply this to tongues or to any of the other eighteen spiritual gifts, for God distributes these gifts in the body as He wills.

If you have never spoken in tongues, don't worry about it — just keep concentrating on using whatever other gift or gifts God has given you. If you do have the gift of tongues, praise God for it, but do not feel proud of yourself or require it of your brother. If you do, you are violating the very principle of love which Paul tried so hard to establish in these chapters. You may have the gift, but like the Corinthians, you lack the fruit to make it effective and edifying.

Study Questions

1. Describe the difference between spiritual gifts and spiritual fruit. Give some examples of each.

2. In light of the concept of the "Pentecostal event," why is it wrong to expect that every spiritual Christian should speak in tongues at least once?

3. What arguments are given in the chapter to prove that tongues in First Corinthians (as contrasted to Acts 2, for example) were ecstatic utterances and not known languages? Do you agree with this?

4. List the rules given for the use of tongues and comment on them.

10

No Easter, No Church

I Corinthians 15

WE HAVE BEEN STRESSING all along that the Corinthian Christians were carnal in their attitude toward spiritual things. But this does not mean that they lacked intelligence. Probably a good many of the church members were well-versed in philosophy, and could debate with the best of them. All Greeks admired wisdom and knowledge.

DIFFICULTY

The transition from Greek philosophy to Christian theology was not always an easy process for many of the Corinthians. It would have been hard even if they were spiritual Christians, but their carnality accentuated the problem. It "puffed them up" (8:1) and gave them what might be called an intellectual superiority complex. They had the idea that they were smart enough to adjust Christian teachings to suit themselves.

This was the root of this particular difficulty, because one of the Christian teachings the Corinthians decided to revamp in light of their contemporary philosophy was that of the resurrection of the dead. No doubt they had good intentions, and they probably thought they were doing Christianity a favor. They thought that the best way to evangelize what

they might have called the "first-century man" was to gear the
message to his thought patterns. (I am aware, to be sure,
that the custom of counting years from the birth of Christ
was not introduced until the sixth century, but this sounds
sufficiently like "twentieth-century man" to make us see the
point.) They probably thought, just as we do today, that
man had "come of age" at that time. What they didn't realize at first, however, was that by tampering with the doctrine of the resurrection of the dead, they were threatening
to pull the rug out from under the Christian faith in general.

Before moving into the details of this Corinthian heresy,
it should be pointed out that if you run back through church
history, you find the same thing happening time after time.
While it is good to adapt your manner of expressing Christian doctrine to contemporary thought patterns and vocabu-
lary, it is dangerous to allow the contemporary world to
change the essence of the doctrines you are trying to communicate. But this is just how many heresies start. Once
theologians in any age set about the task of standing judgment over God's revelation, they begin a deteriorating process which has no limits.

This kind of theological approach makes Christian theology a reed blowing in the wind. One has to keep up with
the theological headlines to find out what Christians believe
from day to day. Just a short time ago, for example, the
God-is-dead theology was becoming so popular that a secular magazine like *Time* had to do a cover story on it. That
has gone by the board and now people are clustering around
what is called the "theology of hope." Yesterday it was
Rauschenbusch's "social gospel," today it is Cox's "secular
city." Tomorrow it may be a Marxoid "theology of revolution."

Instead of accepting at face value what God has revealed
through the Scriptures, many theologians approach the Bible like a schoolmaster with his hickory stick, anxious to
criticize and correct. They feel that theology is basically not
a series of statements derived from propositional revelation
and divine inspiration, but rather of enlightened human feel-

ing or reasoning, tempered by the culture in which the theology is developed. Since we live in a cultural situation different from that of the Biblical authors, we should expect to modify our theology accordingly. One implication of the Corinthians' carnality was that they allowed culture to mold theology rather than attempting to let Biblical revelation mold both culture and theology. The result of this mentality, whether in the first century or in the twentieth is not Christianity, but a dangerous syncretism.

People today are not so much concerned about individual salvation or the afterlife, says Dietrich Bonhoeffer, for example. He therefore develops what he calls a "religionless Christianity" which shows more concern for the problems of this world than for the world to come. Since we live in a world which is becoming more secularized every day, adds Harvey Cox, we also should secularize our theology. At times it seems that men like Cox are saying that God speaks to man more clearly through secular society than He does through the Bible.

Coming back to the Corinthians, we can now appreciate the fact that their error amounted to more or less the same thing. Paul had preached that Christ had risen from the dead and that all the dead would ultimately participate in the resurrection. This doctrine did not fit in well with the Greek mentality, the "first-century man." When Paul preached in Athens they listened to him attentively until he came to the doctrine of the resurrection. Then they laughed him to scorn (Acts 17:32). Their philosophical orientation was basically dualistic. They believed in eternal forces of good and evil. What was spiritual was for them on the good side, but what was material was on the bad side. It was all right to believe that man's spirit would go to heaven, but his body? That was matter! Many Greeks tried to divorce their true spiritual selves from their bodies, postulating that what they did with their bodies was not related to what they did in their spirits. Some went one way and became hedonists by indulging their bodies and some went the opposite way and became ascetics by denying their bodies. They were all happy to think that when their souls went to heaven they finally would be free of their material bodies. It was not good news to them that on some future day they would have to take their bodies back again.

In the light of this, the Corinthians tried to modify Christian theology. But it didn't go over very well with Paul. They might have had all good intentions in making Christianity more relevant to "first-century man," but in doing so they had fallen into serious heresy.

DOCTRINE

Paul knew that the entire Christian religion is dependent on what one believes about the resurrection: "But if Christ is preached, that He was raised from the dead, how is it that some of you claim there is no resurrection of the dead?" (15:12). As you read First Corinthians 15, keep in mind that Paul does not accuse the Corinthians of denying the bodily resurrection of Christ Himself. If they knowingly did this, they couldn't have become Christians in the first place. But whereas they accepted the resurrection of Christ, they denied the resurrection of the rest of humanity. Paul shows the fallacy of this in three major divisions of his doctrinal section:

1. *The resurrection in the past — a historical fact* (15: 1-11). Easter is an absolute necessity for the Christian faith. The historical evidence that Christ was raised bodily from the dead is reviewed here by Paul, and presented as conclusive. Peter, the twelve apostles, James, and then five hundred eyewitnesses testified firsthand to the fact. Many unbelievers have tried to throw up a curtain of suspicion around the historicity of the Resurrection, but without success. The historical evidence for it is every bit as credible as that which tells us that Copernicus discovered the solar system or that Napoleon ruled France.

The basic problem in believing the resurrection of Christ lies not so much in the credibility of the historical facts which prove it, as in the moral demands which immediately face a person who accepts the fact. The resurrection proves that Christ is Lord. Christ demands of all men repentance from sin and spiritual regeneration which amounts to an entire moral revolution. Unfortunately, most people still prefer to practice sin rather than submit themselves to Christ as Lord and allow Him to transform their lives. In order to assuage their uneasy consciences, they attack Christianity. Naturally they pitch their attack on a rational or historical plane to avoid the moral dimension which is their real problem. If all men faced the historical evidence for the resurrection without moral prejudice, many more would realize that Christ actually did rise from the dead, and consequently many more would be saved.

2. *The resurrection in the present — an article of faith* (15:12-19). Once Paul reaffirms the historicity of Christ's resurrection, he moves on to the resurrection of the rest of humanity which was the main problem for the Corinthians. The two are really tied up in the same package, although the Corinthians did not realize this. They wanted one without the other. If, as the Corinthians supposed, the dead did not rise, then Christ could not have risen either (15:13, 16). Paul's chilling conclusion reads: "If Christ has not been raised, then your faith is futile; you are still in your sins" (15:17).

The people of Paul's day were concerned about their future life. They lived in a restless age; they needed a certainty on which to latch and they sought it in a religious belief in the afterlife. Paul offered them this certainty: "If we have hope in Christ for this life only, then of all people we are most to be pitied" (15:19). But the joyful witness of the apostles was that since they had seen the risen Jesus, they knew that the resurrection was more than mere wishful thinking. Nor was it an optional Christian belief. It was part of the fabric of Christianity.

3. *The resurrection in the future — a blessed expectation* (15:20-57). Biblically, the resurrection is a two-sided coin: a glorious event for believers but a bitter tragedy for unbelievers. According to Jesus there is a "resurrection of life"

and a "resurrection of judgment" (John 5:29). As surely as Christ rose from the dead historically all men will rise from the dead in the future. The "first resurrection" (Rev. 20:5, 6) is that of the believer and the "second resurrection" (Rev. 20:11-15) of the unbeliever. Those who ignore this Biblical teaching do so at their own personal risk.

One of the most fascinating passages in this chapter is 15:23, 24 which says: "each, to be sure, in his turn: Christ first, then His own at His coming. After that the end will come, when He hands over the kingdom to God the Father, after abolishing every ruler and all government and power." The resurrection of the believers or the first resurrection apparently is not a single event, but according to this passage it is a composite of three events: one already past now and two in the future. Since this involves a delicate interpretation of prophecy, some readers might not be in agreement, but nevertheless, it merits consideration.

The first part of the first resurrection took place when Christ Himself rose from the dead ("Christ first"). This is described in some detail in Matthew 27:52, 53: "the tombs were opened and many bodies of the buried saints were raised and after His resurrection they left their tombs, entered the holy city and appeared to many."

Who were *they?* It seems that they must have been all the saints who had trusted God from the time of Adam to the time of Christ's resurrection. They had been saved by promise, but they had not yet been fully redeemed because Christ's blood had not yet been shed for them on the cross. This fits in with Peter's puzzling statement that Christ "went and preached to the spirits in prison" (I Peter 3:19), and Paul's assertion that Christ descended into hell and when "He ascended on high, He led the captured away into captivity" (Eph. 4:8-10). The message Christ preached to Abraham, Moses, David, Jeremiah, and others in Hades was simply, "It is finished!" This is what they had been waiting for: their promised redemption was now complete. They rose from the dead on that first Easter day along with their Lord.

The second part of the first resurrection will take place "at

Christ's coming." This is the rapture of the church, described in more detail in 15:51, 52. All living believers shall be changed instantly, and the dead believers shall also rise. First Thessalonians 4:13-18 adds the fact that the dead will rise first. All those who have been born again from the time of Christ's resurrection until the rapture will be included in this event.

The third part of the first resurrection will occur after the millennium when Christ "shall have delivered up the kingdom to the Father." Exactly who will or will not be included at this time is not clear, but undoubtedly those born during the millennium who trust Christ will be among them. This concludes the first resurrection and at this time all believers of all ages will have received their bodies once again.

DECISION

Since their error concerning the resurrection was the only major doctrinal aberration in which the Corinthians were involved, Paul naturally places his emphasis predominantly on theology in this chapter. Although he doesn't say it in so many words, Paul's decision would be: you already believe in Christ's resurrection, believe also what He taught you about the resurrection of all the dead. If you don't, you will soon find that you have built your theology on sand, and that the first strong wave of opposition will wash it away.

Finally, Paul goes on to make a practical application of this doctrine. In the last two verses of the chapter he reminds the Corinthians that good doctrine will result in good life. Psychologists tell us that one of the most powerful human instincts is that of self-preservation. This creates a certain fear of death, which can be devastating to the integration of the human personality if not adequately handled. The man who conquers his fear of death is usually a happy and well-adjusted man. Through his confidence not only in Christ's resurrection, but also in the certainty of his own, Paul had so overcome this fear that he called death a "victory" (15:55).

Paul knows that if we hold a strong doctrine of the resurrection we will reap the same personal benefits. This in
turn will give us the basis for living lives that are "steadfast,
immovable, at all times abounding in the Lord's service" (15:
58).

Study Questions

1. Explain in your own words why Greek philosophy would
turn the Corinthians against the doctrine of the resurrection.

2. Why do modern secular theologians play down the resurrection? In what way do they think they are helping Christianity?
Do you agree?

3. Is the resurrection of the dead an optional element in a
statement of faith for a Bible-believing Christian? What Biblical
evidence do you have for your answer?

4. Distinguish between the three parts of the first resurrection. What is meant by the second resurrection?

11

The Testimony of Social Service

I Corinthians 16:1-4

SOMEONE HAS RATHER PLAYFULLY asked whether Paul might have taken a coffee break between chapters 15 and 16!

Chapter 15 builds up to a stirring climax which raises the reader into the heavenlies. The lofty thoughts of resurrection, rapture, the victory of death, immortality, and the victory through our Lord Jesus Christ are the makings of an exhilarating religious experience. One tends to feel that he is in orbit, floating comfortably in the zero gravity of space.

But chapter 16? "With regard to the collection for the saints" is like the shock of re-entry. To return to earth from outer space is a jolting experience, and when Paul changes the subject from resurrection to finances, the sensitive reader feels it.

Christianity is like this, however. The faithful Christian can never forget that he is a citizen of two worlds. In one place, Paul reminds Christians that they must be subject to "governing authorities" and pay "tax to whom tax is due" (Rom. 13:1, 7). In another place, Paul declares that "our citizenship belongs in heaven" (Phil. 3:20). A Christian has serious responsibilities in this world and also in the world to come.

Until recent years, evangelical Christians tended to go to an extreme in their otherworldliness. This was not always true, however, since evangelicals in the eighteenth and nineteenth centuries were often on the frontiers of social reform. But it is true generally of the first half of the twentieth century. Evangelicals, unfortunately, overreacted to the triple threat of liberalism, evolution, and the social gospel which jeopardized Biblical Christianity for many years. Within the past ten or fifteen years, however, evangelicals have overcome their inferiority complex and, while they haven't embraced the new secular theology, they have listened to it enough to decide that it is time to relate the social responsibility of the Christian to evangelical theology.

Difficulty

For many years I read First Corinthians 16:1-4 without realizing that it is a passage on social service. The same applies to Second Corinthians 8 and 9, a passage to which we must make frequent reference if we are fully to understand Paul's teaching on the subject. Having been oriented to contemporary church economics, I used to read these passages with the erroneous idea that they referred to some principles that churches should adopt to finance themselves.

I wasn't alone in this mistake. Not one of the collection of commentaries I have on First Corinthians develops this passage in the context of social service. The inference is that the offerings Paul speaks of were for the church itself. Commentators recognize the fact that Paul referred to the offering for the poor at Jerusalem, but most sermons on these texts have not attempted to arouse a sense of responsibility for the poor of our own day, but rather to increase the amount of money in the offering plates.

For the Corinthians this could not have been the purpose at all. The Corinthian church had few, if any, financial needs as a church organization. It met in the house of one of the members, so there was no rent, taxes, or maintenance cost. The modern idea of a full-time, fully-supported pastor had not been thought of, so they had no pastors' salary, telephone bill, or automobile expenses to be concerned about. There were no Sunday school materials, no hymnals, and no church bus. We have no evidence that offerings were taken up in the church. They didn't even have a church treasurer or give financial reports.

Paul's appeal to the Corinthians for funds had nothing to do with expenses at Corinth. It was for Jerusalem; not for the Jerusalem church expenses, but rather to help the poor people there in a material way. This is a major Biblical principle; *giving on the part of Christians should be basically for others.*

Specifically, what was this all about?

The Jerusalem Christians were poorer than most in those days. The region had suffered a famine (Acts 11:27, 28) which had impoverished many — Christians and non-Christians alike. But other factors as well had made Jerusalem poor as cities went in the ancient world. The Jews in the outside world supported the city with subsidies, much as they do today.

The Christians, however, would benefit little from this subsidy that came into Jerusalem. The anti-Christian persecution that began at the time of the martyrdom of Stephen drove many from the city itself and forced the others to form a sort of ghetto. We have no evidence that all the Christians in Jerusalem were poor, but evidently if there were any wealthy ones, they could not help enough by themselves. Augustine conjectured that the experiment in communal living which was attempted in the Jerusalem church had contributed to their poverty.

In any case, the Jerusalem church seems, from the Biblical evidence, to have been an introverted church. The outreach of the church is attributed largely to the unwelcome force of persecution, and their well-entrenched opposition to taking the Gospel to the Gentiles comes through in the Book of Acts. Like many churches today, it seems that they would have been content if they were the only Christians in the world. A church that sows sparingly will also reap sparingly.

Just the opposite attitude characterized the church at Antioch to the north. Rather than being introverted, Antioch was a centrifugal church, a church for others. When the first

news of the famine in Jerusalem came, the brethren there decided to send relief. They were conscious of their obligation
for social service, so they sent Paul and Barnabas with the
offerings (Acts 11:29, 30). Not only were they involved in
the testimony of social service, but they also were the greatest missionary church in the New Testament.

On his first furlough, Paul had agreed to raise funds for
social service. After the Jerusalem Council, the brethren sent
Paul and Barnabas out to the Gentiles once again, "Only
they wanted us to remember the needy, which I myself was
eager to do" (Gal. 2:9, 10). Paul couldn't do much to fulfill his promise on his second term. He was busy founding
the churches which later would be able to contribute. He
kept his priorities straight. First of all churches must be
planted, then encouraged to participate in social service.
Some today make the error of beginning with social service
and imagining that churches will result. Social service is
never an adequate substitute for evangelism.

By the time his third term came around, Paul was prepared to do something concrete for the poor. The churches
were established and able to move into a social service program. The first mention of Paul's efforts is found here in the
passage we are studying.

In Second Corinthians 8:1, 2 we find that the churches of
Macedonia (Philippi, Berea, Thessalonica, etc.) had
responded to Paul's appeal, and on that basis he expects the
Corinthian church to contribute. His policy for fund raising
is interesting at this point, since he does not hesitate to make
comparisons between those who give and those who don't,
setting up as good examples the churches of Macedonia.
Later on, when Corinth had also contributed, he uses Macedonia and Achaia (Corinth) to convince the brethren in
Rome that they should give also (Rom. 15:26).

DOCTRINE

In his doctrinal section, Paul expounds the great principles of giving. His starting point is that giving should be

primarily for others. He that sows liberally will also reap liberally, he says in another place (II Cor. 9:6). Whether the outreach of the church involves the spiritual dimension of evangelism, or the material dimension of social service, the motive of giving should be for others. A church which gives only for itself will soon be a stagnant church. Philippi was a church for others, while Corinth was a church for itself. Look at the problems in the Corinthian church! Antioch was a church for others, while Jerusalem was a church for itself. Introversion is a sign of carnality in the church.

Even today, you show me a truly missionary-minded church, and I'll show you a live church being blessed of God in all ways. Many churches make the mistake of considering their missionary program as a sideline or relegating it to the women's missionary society. This is fatal. Missions should be foremost with operating expenses the sideline. The minimum goal for any church should be 51% of its budget for others.

But when you agree that your goal should be for others, the next question is: which others? Just exactly who are those whom the church should help?

Biblically, it seems that the "others" are basically other Christians. It is interesting to see how *diakonía* (social service) is tied up closely with *koinonía* (Christian fellowship) in these passages. In both Second Corinthians 8:4 and 9:13 they are used in the same verses. "Most urgently begging of us (*koinonía*) the favor of taking part in this service (*diakonía*) to the saints" (8:4). "Because of the proof of this service (*diakonía*) they are praising God for your loyalty to the good news about Christ which you confess, and for the liberality of your contribution (*koinonía*) for them and for all" (9:13). The primary reference in these and other passages is to the "saints" but "to all men" is also included.

While the Bible commands us to carry our social testimony to unbelievers, *diakonía* is prescribed first for believers. "So then, as opportunity offers, let us practice what is beneficial for everyone, *but particularly toward the members of the family of faith*" (Gal. 6:10). Social service should move out in three concentric circles. The first responsibility of the Christian is for his own family ("Whoever does not provide for his dependents, and specially for his own family, has denied the faith and is worse than an unbeliever" (I Tim. 5:8). Secondly, the Christian is responsible for the "family of faith," and finally to society in general.

To what point should you help others? It is certain that the church cannot make much of an impression on the poor segments of our society. As Ron James says, "The church will not have the resources, not in a million years, to fill the almost bottomless chasms of human need, but it has a command to identify with men, to share their suffering, and thereby to make the incarnation visible."

On the other hand, it is equally certain that the church, especially in the United States, can do much more for others than it is doing now. The Bible says, "When we have food and clothing, we shall be content with these" (I Tim. 6:8). Most of us are not content with sufficient food and raiment, and we might as well admit it. Some Christians sacrifice materially in order to devote their resources to others, but they are not as numerous as they should be today.

If it is true that *diakonía* (social service) to the world of unbelievers is secondary, what is primary? It is the *kerygma,* or evangelization. If resources for the world are limited, the best investment of them is in enterprises which will multiply churches and bring multitudes into the kingdom of God. Feeding the hungry is important as a social witness, but it becomes dangerous if the salvation of men and women is sidetracked by it.

One thorny question remains. Is social service an end or a means to an end? Do we measure social service by suffering relieved or by souls saved? Some are reluctant to participate in social service if it is not justified as another evangelistic tool. This seems to be an error. The Good Samaritan was not said to have been interested in making the wounded man a Samaritan at that point. When Jesus healed the ten lepers, he rejoiced that one returned. But his *diakonía* was not only 10 percent successful because all didn't return. It was 100 percent successful because all were healed. Whereas all is done "in the name of the Lord" and whereas the angels rejoice if a soul is saved through it, our social service is an end in itself. Whenever we relieve human suffering or promote justice, we have been successful in social service.

DECISION

In developing the doctrine of giving for social service, we have deviated considerably from our text in First Corinthians 16:1-4. In this concluding section, let us draw some principles of giving from these verses, taking them as Paul's decision in this case.

The first principle is that the needs are clearly and precisely made known (16:1). Paul was raising money for the poor Christians of Jerusalem, and he was not reticent to tell the Corinthians that he needed money for them. This is incongruous with the attitude (which is rapidly disappearing) of some Christians today that needs should be made known only to God and not to fellow Christians.

Some have objected that here Paul is raising money for others, but if it were for himself, he would not have been so specific. Wrong! Paul makes a direct appeal to the Roman church for travel funds for himself when he says, "Whenever I might travel to Spain, I do hope to see you with my own eyes on passing through, and to have an escort from you (financial help?) on the way, after first having enjoyed your fellowship for a while" (Romans 15:24).

A second principle is that Paul solicits funds authoritatively. "I commanded the churches," he says (I Cor. 16:1). There is no hesitation or apology for raising money. Many of our churches today would do well to encourage this type of appeal, rather than the indirect methods of fund raising that have departed so far from the Scriptures.

After setting forth the need, Paul did not hesitate to propose some efficient plans to aid human weakness in this area. He pushed for more systematic giving, knowing that this would result in more total quantity in the long run. He was pragmatic enough to expect results. "When the first day of each week comes, let each of you set aside," he says. Paul probably wasn't referring to the church offering on Sunday morning, as we are prone to think. We have already seen that in all probability there was no such thing in Corinth as a Sunday offering. He was telling the Corinthians that they should save their money systematically. If they did, there would be no reason for him to push for further collections when he arrived, because the quantity would have been adequate.

Modern methods of giving, such as envelopes, mailed reminders, and faith promise cards are not carnal as some imagine. Whatever helps us to be more systematic about fulfilling what we have already determined in our hearts is good in the church.

Finally, Paul expected the Corinthians to give a proportion of their income to the Lord. All Jews knew that the tithe, or ten percent of their income, was what was required by God. It was required not only under the law, but before the law with Abraham. Christians may not be bound by the law, but they should be ashamed if they do not do at least as well as the Jews, by giving their tithe. This is the minimum. Some members of the body of Christ have a charismatic gift of liberality (Rom. 12:8), which enables them to give far and above the average. This is a special privilege, and should be exercised by those who have it. Paul refers to it in Second Corinthians 8:7, "be foremost in this gracious work also."

The example of Christ is the touchstone of all teaching on Christian giving. "Although He was rich, yet He became poor for your sakes, so that you by His poverty might become rich" (II Cor. 8:9). Christ gave Himself for others. He came to save, and He came to heal. The proper balance between the spiritual and the social was not a problem for Him. If the churches today imitated His example, they might find themselves with a clearer and more effective testimony in the world.

Study Questions

1. What evidence do we have that the passage on giving (16: 1-4) is related to social service?

2. How could your church become more involved in social service? Do you think the social activities of a church should be directed primarily to the community in general or to Christians who are needy?

3. Do you believe that Christian social service is a means toward some other end (such as evangelism) or that it is an end in itself?

4. Should tithing be practiced today? How extensively is it practiced among your friends who are Christians? Is there a better way of raising money in your church?

12

What the Spirit Says to the Churches

FOR MOST OF US TODAY it is not hard to identify in many ways with the Corinthian believers and our churches with the church there. Dr. D. Martyn Lloyd-Jones has said that First Corinthians is the most relevant book of the Bible to contemporary life in the West. It probably did not acquire its relevance just lately, however. Chances are that through the ages church after church has called it a contemporary book. The different matters touched in the epistle are problems that any Christian in any place and during any century might face.

This did not happen by accident. The Holy Spirit inspired Paul to give the type of counsel to a young church that would help Christians throughout the history of the church. On the Isle of Patmos John wrote while the Lord dictated letters to seven other churches. Each one ended with the words: "Whoever has an ear, let him hear what the Spirit says to the churches." This is a fitting admonition also for the conclusion of First Corinthians.

The Spirit will not force His way on anyone. He can speak to you, and you can refuse to listen. You can disobey Him; you can quench Him. But if your heart is open, He will gently drive the truth of God home and change your life through it. Through the Spirit's application of First Corinthians you can find new power and effectiveness as a Christian. And if a good number of the members of your church all decide to hear what the Spirit says, this book can turn your church on. New life can pour in, Christians can straighten out twisted lives, carnality can disappear, gifts can be discovered and used, the church can grow, and your community can know that Christ is Lord!

In general, the message of the Spirit through First Corinthians is that carnality in the church must be conquered. When a person commits himself to Christ the break with the world must be complete. Worldliness can drag your church down and reduce its effectiveness to zero. The Corinthians thought they could toy around with a compromise with the world and through it be more useful to Christ. It didn't work then and it won't work now. The world does not respect the church more because she identifies herself more with the world. There is nothing like a clean-cut stand for Christ and a separated life.

A fad has developed in some circles called "making the church relevant." This futile attempt to make salvation more palatable to sinners is as old as the Corinthians. As Harold Lindsell says, "Ultimately the Gospel is relevant to the true needs of men and for us to try to debase the good coinage of the Gospel by vitiating it so that we can make it more attractive to men is to lose the Gospel and to make it irrelevant."

Christ's church is in the world today to change the world. Woe to the church which allows the world to dominate her and ultimately make her over in its image! But this is the trouble with many of our churches. The Spirit says, kill carnality! Know God's will as revealed in the Bible, and trust the Holy Spirit to apply the truth in daily life. Live according to the rules that God has set down for His family. Ten of those rules are set forth in First Corinthians. In review, here they are:

1. Beware of carrying your worldly ways of life into your church. The Corinthians split their church because they dragged the party spirit of the world in. They squabbled with each other and lost the visible unity of the Body of

Christ that God demands. If this happens to you, bury your self-pride and reconcile yourself to your brother.

2. Don't tolerate sin in your church — deal with it. Sexual impurity is only one of the many sins that can cripple churches if they are not cared for. When a brother persists in sin, try to make him repent and change his ways. If all else fails, excommunicate him before he contaminates the entire congregation.

3. Follow God's principles for a well-adjusted married life and a well-adjusted single life. Sex can be a great blessing in your life or a terrible curse. Only by following God's rules can you fully enjoy sex and marriage. If you violate them, you are in for disappointment and a perturbed life.

4. Be tolerant of the views of your brother on amoral issues. He may do things you wouldn't do or vice versa. Allow latitude in your church on these problems. The weak should not judge the strong, nor should the strong look down on the weak as fanatics.

5. Insist that women recognize that they should be submissive to men. This applies equally to the family and the church. When women forget their place in the order of creation, trouble for everyone is right around the corner.

6. Maintain a deep reverence in your worship services. God can be worshiped in many different ways, each as effective as the other, but do not let carnality bring into your services elements and attitudes which will nullify your worship, especially at the Lord's Table.

7. Discover your gift or gifts and use them to the fullest extent possible. Work as a team, each member with his own gift in harmony with the other members. If every member of your church begins to use one or more gifts, you will have a complete renovation before you know it.

8. If you speak in tongues, follow the rules. If you don't speak in tongues, do not be concerned. Like other gifts, God chooses the people He gives them to, and if He has not given you the gift of tongues, He has given you some other gift which He expects you to use.

9. Anchor your faith on the rock of the doctrine of resur-

rection. The resurrection of Christ is a solid fact. On that basis we are assured that we will all rise from the dead and receive our bodies once again. This belief helps make us victorious Christians.

10. Balance the internal financial needs of your church with outreach, both evangelism and social service. The church for others is the church which God blesses.

Paul knew well that if they would listen to what the Spirit said to the church through him, the Corinthians would soon overcome their multiple problems and become a powerhouse for God in the world. Your church could do the same.

> Keep your eyes open for spiritual danger; stand true to the Lord; act like men; be strong; and whatever you do, do it with kindness and love.
>
> (I Cor. 16:13, 14, Living N.T.)

Study Questions

1. Discuss the true relationship of the church with the world. How much should the church be like the world in order to be "relevant"?

2. Victory over carnality is a key to good health in any church. Show how carnality can produce each one of the ten major problems mentioned in this chapter.

3. How could each of those problems be solved if carnality were overcome?

4. Which of these difficulties are found in your church to one degree or another? Suggest some contemporary solutions. If this question produces the desired results, studying this book has been worthwhile!